C000259475

Norwegian
Phrase Book
&
Dictionary

Berlitz Publishing
New York   Munich   Singapore

Contacting the Editors
Every effort has been made to provide accurate information in this publication, but changes are inevitable. The publisher cannot be responsible for any resulting loss, inconvenience or injury. We would appreciate it if readers would call our attention to any errors or outdated information. We also welcome your suggestions; if you come across a relevant expression not in our phrase book, please contact us: Berlitz Publishing, 193 Morris Avenue, Springfield, NJ 07081, USA. Email: comments@berlitzbooks.com

First Printing: May 2008
Printed in Singapore

Publishing Director: Sheryl Olinsky Borg
Senior Editor/Project Manager: Lorraine Sova
Norwegian Editorial: Kjell Bjørnskau, Morten Abildsnes
Cover Design: Claudia Petrilli
Interior Design: Derrick Lim, Juergen Bartz
Production Manager: Elizabeth Gaynor
Composition: Datagrafix, Inc.
Cover Photo: © Art Kowalsky/Alamy
Interior Photos: p. 14 © Studio Fourteen/Brand X Pictures/age fotostock; p. 18 © 2007 Jupiterimages Corporation, © Sergey Chushkin/2003-2007 Shutterstock, Inc.; p. 25 © Pixtal/age fotostock; p. 33 © Roman Korchuk, 2006/Shutterstock, Inc.; p. 37 © Corbis/fotosearch.com; p. 47 © Purestock/Alamy; p. 52 © Quendi Language Services; p. 55 © Stockbyte Photography/2002-07 Veer Incorporated; p. 68 © Quendi Language Services; p. 81 © Javier Larrea/Pixtal/age fotostock; p. 83 © Netfalls/2003-2007 Shutterstock, Inc.; p. 98 © Iain Davidson Photographic/Alamy; p. 101 © Imageshop.com; p. 105 © image100/Corbis; p. 108 © TongRo Image Stock/Alamy; p. 112 © TongRo Image Stock/Alamy; p. 114 © 2007 Jupiterimages Corporation; p. 123 © Iconotec/Alamy; p. 131 © Carsten Medom Madsen/Shutterstock, Inc.; p. 139 © Jupiterimages/Brand X/Corbis; p. 141 © Stockbyte/Fotosearch.com; p. 143 © Corbis/2006 JupiterImages Corporation; p.146 © David McKee/2003-2007 Shutterstock, Inc.; p. 147, 150, 165 © 2007 Jupiterimages Corporation; inside back cover: © H.W.A.C.

Contents

Pronunciation 7
  Consonants 7
  Vowels 9

Vowel Combinations   10
How to Use This Book 12

Survival

Arrival and Departure 15
  ESSENTIAL 15
  Passport Control and
    Customs 15

Money and Banking 16
  ESSENTIAL 16
  ATM, Bank and Currency
    Exchange 17

Transportation 18
  ESSENTIAL 18
  Ticketing 19
  Plane 21
    Getting to the Airport 21
    Check-in and
      Boarding 21
    Luggage 23
    Finding Your Way 23
  Train 23
    Questions 24
    Departures 25
    Boarding 25
  Bus and Train 26
  Subway [Underground] . . 27
  Boat and Ferry 27
  Bicycle and Motorcycle . . 28
  Taxi 28
  Car 30

    Car Rental [Hire] 30
    Gas [Petrol] Station . . 31
    Asking Directions . . . 32
    Parking 33
    Breakdown and
      Repairs 34
    Accidents 34

Accommodations 35
  ESSENTIAL 35
  Finding Lodging 36
  At the Hotel 37
    Price 38
    Questions 38
    Problems 40
    Check-out 41
  Renting 41
    Household Items 42
  Hostel 43
  Camping 44

**Internet and
Communications** 45
  ESSENTIAL 45
  Computer, Internet
    and E-mail 46
  Phone 47
    On the Phone 48
  Fax 50
  Post Office 50

Food

Eating Out 53
  ESSENTIAL 53
  Restaurant Types. 54
  Reservations and
    Questions. 54
  Ordering 56
  Cooking Methods 57
  Special Requirements . . . 57
  Dining with Kids 58
  Complaints 58
  Paying. 59
  Market 60
  Dishes, Utensils and
    Kitchen Tools 61

Meals. 62
  Breakfast. 62
  Appetizers [Starters] 64

Soup 65
Fish and Seafood. 66
Meat and Poultry. 69
Vegetables and Staples . . 72
Spices. 74
Fruit and Nuts 75
Cheese 77
Dessert 77

Drinks 79
  ESSENTIAL 79
  Non-alcoholic Drinks. . . . 80
  Aperitifs, Cocktails and
    Liqueurs. 81
  Beer 82
  Wine 82

Menu Reader. 83

People

Talking. 99
  ESSENTIAL 99
  Communication
    Difficulties 100
  Making Friends 100
  Travel Talk. 102
  Relationships. 102
  Work and School. 103
  Weather 104

Romance. 104
  ESSENTIAL 104
  Making Plans 105
  Pick-up [Chat-up]
    Lines 106
  Accepting and
    Rejecting 106
  Getting Physical. 107
  Sexual Preferences 107

Fun

Sightseeing 109
  ESSENTIAL 109
  Tourist Information
    Office 109
  Tours 110
  Sights 111
  Impressions 112
  Religion 113

Shopping 113
  ESSENTIAL 113
  Stores 115
  Services 116
    Spa 117
    Hair Salon 117
  Sales Help 118
  Preferences 119
  Decisions 119
  Bargaining 120
  Paying 120
  Complaints 121
  Souvenirs 121
  Antiques 124

  Clothing 124
    Color 125
    Clothes and
      Accessories 125
    Fabric 126
    Shoes 127
    Sizes 127
  Newsstand and
    Tobacconist 128
  Photography 128

Sports and Leisure 129
  ESSENTIAL 129
  Spectator Sports 130
  Participating 131
  At the Beach/Pool 131
  Winter Sports 133
  In the Countryside 134

Culture and Nightlife . . . 135
  ESSENTIAL 135
  Entertainment 136
  Nightlife 138

Special Needs

Business Travel 140
  ESSENTIAL 140
  Business
    Communication 140

Travel with Children 142
  ESSENTIAL 142
  Fun with Kids 143

  Basic Needs for Kids . . . 144
  Babysitting 144
  Health and Emergency . . 145

For the Disabled 145
  ESSENTIAL 145
  Getting Help 146

Resources

Emergencies 148
  ESSENTIAL 148

Police 148
  ESSENTIAL 148
  Lost Property and Theft 149

Health 150
  ESSENTIAL 150
  Finding a Doctor 151
  Symptoms 151
  Health Conditions 152
  Hospital 153
  Dentist 153
  Gynecologist 154
  Optician 154
  Payment and Insurance . 154
  Pharmacy [Chemist] . . . 155
  ESSENTIAL 155
    Dosage Instructions . 155
    Health Problem 156

  Basic Needs 156

Reference 158
  Grammar 158
  Numbers 163
    ESSENTIAL 163
    Ordinal Numbers . . . 164
  Time 165
    ESSENTIAL 165
  Days 166
    ESSENTIAL 166
  Dates 166
  Months 166
  Seasons 167
  Holidays 167
  Conversion Tables 168
    Mileage 168
    Measurement 168
    Temperature 169
    Oven Temperature . . 169
  Useful Websites 169

Dictionary

**English-Norwegian
Dictionary** 170

**Norwegian-English
Dictionary** 197

Pronunciation

This section is designed to make you familiar with the sounds of Norwegian—the Oslo accent—by using our simplified phonetic transcription. You'll find the pronunciation of the Norwegian letters explained below, together with their "imitated" equivalents (the Norwegian alphabet is the same as in English, with the addition of the letters æ, ø and å). This system is used throughout the phrase book; simply read the pronunciation as if it were English, noting any special rules below.

Stress has been indicated in the phonetic transcription with underlining, tone with the accent marks and long vowels with bold.

▶ For more on Norwegian tone, see page 11.

▶ For more on Norwegian vowels, see page 9.

Consonants

Letter	Approximate Pronunciation	Symbol	Example	Pronunciation
g	1. before i and y, (sometimes before ei) like y in yes	y	**gi**	y<u>ee</u>
	2. elsewhere, like g in go	g	**gått**	goht
gj	like y in yes	y	**gjest**	yehst
j	like y in yes	y	**ja**	y**ah**
k	1. before i, y and ei like h in hue, but with the tongue raised a little higher	kh	**kino**	<u>khee</u>´·nu
	2. elsewhere, like k in kit	k	**kaffe**	<u>kahf</u>´·fuh
kj	like h in hue, but with the tongue raised a little higher	kh	**kjøre**	<u>khur</u>`·ruh

7

Letter	Approximate Pronunciation	Symbol	Example	Pronunciation
r	rolled near the front of the mouth	r	**rare**	<u>rah</u>`·ruh
s	like s in sit	s	**spise**	s<u>pee</u>`·suh
sj	like sh in shut	sh	**stasjon**	stah·<u>shoo</u>´n
sk	1. before i and y (sometimes before øy), like sh in shut	sh	**ski**	sh<u>ee</u>
	2. elsewhere, like sk in skate	sk	**skole**	<u>skoo</u>`·luh
skj	like sh in shut	sh	**skje**	sheh
w	like v in vice	v	**whisky**	<u>vihs</u>´·kih
z	like s in sit	s	**zoom**	soom

Letters b, c, d, f, h, l, m, n, p, q, t, v, x are generally pronounced as in English.

In Norwegian, consonants are silent in the following situations:
1. The letter **d** is generally silent after **l**, **n** or **r** (e.g. **holde**, **land**, **gård**), and sometimes at the end of words (e.g. **god**, **med**).
2. The letter **g** is silent in the endings **-lig** and **-ig**.
3. The letter **h** is silent when followed by a consonant (e.g. **hjem**, **hva**).
4. The letter **t** is silent in the definite form ("the") of neuter nouns (e.g., **eplet**) and in the pronoun **det**.
5. The letter **v** is silent in certain words (e.g. **selv**, **tolv**, **halv**).
6. In the eastern part of Norway the letter **r** is silent when followed by **l**, **n**, **s**, **t** (and sometimes **d**). These consonants then are pronounced with the tip of the tongue turned up well behind the front teeth. The **r** then ceases to be pronounced, but influences the tone of the following consonant. This "retroflex" pronunciation also occurs in words ending with an **r** if the following word begins with a **d**, **l**, **n**, **s** or **t**.

Vowels

Letter	Approximate Pronunciation	Symbol	Example	Pronunciation
a	1. like a in father, but longer	ah	**tak**	tahk
	2. like a in father	ah	**takk**	tahk
e	1. like e in get, but longer	eh	**sent**	sehnt
	2. like e in get	eh	**penn**	pehn
	3. like a in bad	a	**her**	har
	4. before r, like a in bad	a	**herre**	<u>ha`</u>·ruh
	5. like u in uncle	uh	**sitte**	<u>sih`</u>·tuh
i	1. like ee in bee	ee	**hit**	heet
	2. like i in sit	ih	**sitt**	siht
o	1. like oo in soon, with lips tightly rounded	oo	**ord**	oor
	2. like aw in saw	aw	**tog**	tawg
	3. like u i put, with lips tightly rounded	u	**ost**	ust
	4. like o in cloth	oh	**stoppe**	<u>stohp`</u>·puh
	5. before r, like oo in soon	oo	**hvor**	voor
u	1. like ew in few, but longer	ew	**mur**	mewr
	2. like ew in few	ew	**busk**	bewsk
	3. like u in put, with lips tightly rounded	u	**bukk**	buk
y	1. like ui in fruit, but longer	ui	**myr**	muir
	2. like ui in fruit	ui	**bygge**	<u>buig`</u>·guh

9

Letter	Approximate Pronunciation	Symbol	Example	Pronunciation
æ	1. like a in bad, but longer	a	lære	la`·ruh
	2. like a in bad	a	færre	far´·ruh
ø	1. like ur in fur, but longer and with lips rounded	ur	blø	blur
	2. like ur in fur, with lips rounded	ur	sønn	surn
å	1. like aw in saw, but longer	aw	såpe	saw`·puh
	2. like o in cloth	oh	gått	goht

Vowel Combinations

Letter	Approximate Pronunciation	Symbol	Example	Pronunciation
ai	like ie in tie	ie	mais	mies
au	like ev in ever	ev	sau	sev
ei	like ay in say	ay	geit	yayt
eg	at the end of a word and before n, like ay in say	ay	jeg	yay
oi	like oi in oil	oi	koie	koi`·uh
øy	like ur + y	ury	høy	hury

In Norwegian, vowel length distinguishes meaning. All vowels come in two lengths, long and short. Long vowels are in bold throughout the phonetics.

Norwegian is a tonal language. This means that tone is used to distinguish between certain words, which otherwise would sound the same. For example:

hender (<u>hehn´</u>·nuhr), tone 1 = plural of **hånd** (hand)
hender (<u>hehn`</u>·nuhr), tone 2 = present tense of **hende** (happen)

In the phonetics, tone 1, which is a rising tone (i.e., starts low and rises in pitch) is marked with the acute accent (´); tone 2, which is a falling tone (i.e., starts high and lowers in pitch), with the grave accent (`).

How to Use This Book

These essential phrases can also be heard on the audio CD.

Sometimes you see two alternatives in italics, separated by a slash. Choose the one that's right for your situation.

Essential

I'm here on *vacation [holiday]/business*.

Jeg er her *på ferie/i forretninger.* yay ar har *paw feh´r·yuh/ih fohr·reht´·nihng·uhr*

I'm going to...

Jeg reiser til... yay <u>rays</u>·uhr tihl...

I'm staying at the... Hotel.

Jeg bor på Hotell... yay boor paw hu·<u>tehl´</u>...

You May See...

BUSSHOLDEPLASS/TRIKKEHOLDEPLASS   bus stop/tram stop
INNGANG/UTGANG   enter/exit
STEMPLE BILLETTEN   stamp your ticket

ATM, Bank and Currency Exchange

Where's...?

Hvor er det...? voor <u>a</u>r deh...

– the ATM

– **en minibank** ehn <u>mee´</u>·nih·bangk

– the bank

– **en bank** ehn bahngk

– the currency exchange office

– **et vekslingskontor** eht <u>vehk`s</u>·lihngs·k<u>u</u>n·**too**r

Words you may see are shown in *You May See* boxes.

Any of the words or phrases preceded by dashes can be plugged into the sentence above.

12

Norwegian phrases appear in red.

Read the simplified pronunciation as if it were English. For more on pronunciation, see page 7.

Relationships

Are you married?	**Er du gift?** ar dew yihft
I'm…	**Jeg er…** yay ar…
– single	**– singel** <u>ew</u>`·yift
– in a relationship	**– opptatt** <u>ohp</u>´·taht
– married	**– gift** yift
– divorced	**– skilt** shihlt
– separated	**– separert** seh·pah·<u>reh</u>´rt
I'm widowed.	**Jeg er *enkemann*♂/*enke*♀.** yay ar *ehng*`·kuh·mahn♂/*ehng*´·kuh♀

When different gender forms apply, the masculine form is followed by ♂; feminine by ♀.

▶ For Norwegian pronouns, see page 160.

The arrow indicates a cross reference where you'll find related phrases.

Information boxes contain relevant country, culture and language tips.

Norwegians tend to get right to business and don't engage in much small talk or socializing. You'll find them to be serious and direct in business dealings and in their manner of speaking in general.

You May Hear…

Neste! <u>nehs</u>`·tuh

Billetten/Passet, takk. bil·<u>leht</u>·tuhn/ <u>pahs</u>`·suh tahk

Next!

Your *ticket/passport*, please.

Expressions you may hear are shown in *You May Hear* boxes.

Color-coded side bars identify each section of the book.

13

▼ Survival

▶ **Arrival and Departure**   15
▶ **Money and Banking**   16
▶ **Transportation**   18
▶ **Accommodations**   35
▶ **Internet and Communications**   45

Arrival and Departure

Essential

I'm here on *vacation* [*holiday*]/*business*.	**Jeg er her** *på ferie/i forretninger.* yay ar har *paw feh´r·yuh/ih fohr·reht´·nihng·uhr*
I'm going to…	**Jeg reiser til…** yay rays`·uhr tihl…
I'm staying at the… Hotel.	**Jeg bor på Hotell…** yay boor paw hu·tehl´…

You May Hear…

Billetten/Passet, **takk.** bihl·leht´·tuhn/pahs´·suh tahk	Your *ticket/passport,* please.
Hva er formålet med reisen? vah ar fohr`·maw·luh meh ray`·suhn	What's the purpose of your trip?
Hvor skal du bo? voor skahl dew boo	Where are you staying?
Hvor lenge blir du? voor lehng`·uh bleer dew	How long are you staying?
Hvem reiser du sammen med? vehm ray`·suhr dew sahm´·muhn meh	Who are you with?

Passport Control and Customs

I'm just passing through.	**Jeg er bare på gjennomreise.** yay ar bah`·ruh paw yehn`·nohm·ray·suh
I would like to declare…	**Jeg vil gjerne fortolle…** yay vihl ya`r·nuh fohr·tohl´·luh…
I have nothing to declare.	**Jeg har ingenting å fortolle.** yay hahr ihng`·uhn·tihng aw fohr·tohl´·luh

Har du noe å fortolle? hahr dew <u>noo</u>`·uh aw
fohr·<u>tohl</u>´·luh

Do you have anything to declare?

Du må betale toll for dette. dew maw
buh·<u>tah</u>´·luh tohl fohr <u>deht</u>`·tuh

You must pay duty on this.

Vær så snill å åpne denne bagen. var saw
snihl aw <u>aw</u>`p·nuh <u>dehn</u>`·nuh <u>behg</u>´·guhn

Please open this bag.

Money and Banking

Essential

Where's...?

Hvor er det...? voor ar deh...

– the ATM

– **en minibank** ehn <u>mee</u>´·nih·bangk

– the bank

– **en bank** ehn bahngk

– the currency exchange office

– **et vekslingskontor** eht
<u>vehk</u>`s·lihngs·kun·<u>too</u>r

What time does the bank *open/close*?

Når *åpner/stenger* banken? nohr
<u>aw</u>`p·nuhr/stehng`·uhr <u>bahng</u>´·kuhn

I'd like to change some *dollars/pounds*.

Jeg vil gjerne veksle noen *dollar/ pund*. yay vihl <u>ya</u>`r·nuh <u>vehk</u>`s·luh <u>noo</u>`·uhn
<u>dohl</u>´·lahr/pewn

I'd like to cash a traveler's check [cheque].

Jeg vil gjerne løse inn en reisesjekk. yay
vihl <u>ya</u>`r·nuh <u>lur</u>`·suh ihn ehn <u>ray</u>`·suh·shehk

16

ATM, Bank and Currency Exchange

Can I exchange foreign currency here?	**Kan jeg veksle utenlandsk valuta her?** kahn yay vehk`s·luh **ew**`·tuhn·lahnsk vah·lew´·tah har
What's the exchange rate?	**Hva er vekslingskursen?** vah ar vehk`s·lihngs·**kewr**·suhn
How much is the fee?	**Hvor mye tar dere i kommisjon?** voor **muî**·uh tahr deh`·ruh ih ku·mih·**shoo**´n
I've lost my traveler's checks [cheques].	**Jeg har mistet reisesjekkene.** yay hahr mihs`·tuht ray`·suh·shehk·kuh·nuh
My card was lost.	**Jeg har mistet kortet.** yay hahr mihs`·tuht kohr´·tuh
My credit cards have been stolen.	**Kredittkortene mine ble stjålet.** kreh·**diht**´·kohr·tuh·nuh **mee**´·nuh bleh **styaw**`·luht
My card doesn't work.	**Kortet virker ikke.** kohr´·tuh vihr`·kuhr ihk`·kuh

▶ For numbers, see page 163.

Cash can be obtained from **minibank** (ATMs), which are located throughout Norway. Some debit cards and most major credit cards are accepted. Be sure you know your PIN and whether it is compatible with European machines, which usually accept a four-digit, numeric code. ATMs offer good rates, though there may be hidden fees.

Vekslingskontor (currency exchange offices), banks and post offices are options for exchanging currency. Exchange offices are found at airports, train stations, ship terminals and in many tourist centers. Banks are generally open Monday to Friday 8:15 a.m. to 3:30 p.m., though some close later one day a week and hours may vary in the provinces. Remember to bring your passport, in case you are asked for identification.

You May See...

The Norwegian currency is the **krone** (crown), abbreviated to **kr** or **NOK**, divided into 100 **øre**.

Coins: 50 **øre**; **kr** 1, 5, 10 and 20

Notes: **kr** 50, 100, 200, 500 and 1,000

Transportation

Essential

How do I get to town?	**Hvordan kommer jeg til byen?** <u>voor´</u>·dahn <u>kohm´</u>·muhr yay tihl <u>bui´</u>·uhn
Where is...?	**Hvor er...?** voor ar...
– the airport	– **flyplassen** <u>flui´</u>·plahs·suhn
– the train [railway] station	– **jernbanestasjonen** <u>ya´rn</u>·bah·nuh·stah·shoon·uhn
– the bus station	– **busstasjonen** <u>bews´</u>·stah·shoon·uhn
– the subway [underground] station	– **T-banestasjonen** <u>teh´</u>·bah·nuh·stah·shoon·uhn

How far is it?	**Hvor langt er det?** voor lahngt ar deh
Where can I buy tickets?	**Hvor kan jeg kjøpe billetter?** voor kahn yay khur`·puh bihl·leht´·tuhr
A *one-way [single]/ round-trip [return]* ticket.	**En *enveisbillett/tur-returbillett*.** ehn ehn´·vays·bihl·leht /tewr·reh·tew´r·bil·leht
How much?	**Hvor mye koster det?** voor mui`·uh kohs`·tuhr deh
Are there any discounts?	**Er det noen rabatter?** ar deh noo`·uhn rah·baht´·tuhr
Which…?	**Hvilken…?** vihl´·kuhn…
– gate	– **utgang** ew`t·gahng
– line	– **linje** lihn`·yuh
– platform	– **perrong** pehr·rohng´
Where can I get a taxi?	**Hvor kan jeg få tak i en drosje?** voor kahn yay faw tahk ih ehn drohsh`·uh
Can you take me to this address?	**Kan du kjøre meg til denne adressen?** kahn dew khur`·ruh may tihl dehn`·nuh ahd·rehs´·suhn
Where can I rent a car?	**Hvor kan jeg leie bil?** voor kahn yay lay`·uh beel
Can I have a map?	**Kan jeg få et kart?** kahn yay faw eht kahrt

Ticketing

When's…to Stavanger?	**Når går…til Stavanger?** nohr gawr…tihl stah·vahng´·uhr
– the (first) bus	– **(første) buss** (furrs`·tuh) bews
– the (next) flight	– **(neste) fly** (nehs`·tuh) flui
– the (last) train	– **(siste) tog** (sihs`·tuh) tawg

Where can I buy tickets?	**Hvor kan jeg kjøpe billetter?** voor kahn yay khur`·puh bihl·_leht_´·tuhr
One ticket/Two tickets, please.	**En billett/To billetter, takk.** ehn bihl·_leht_´/**too** bihl·_leht_´·tuhr tak
For *today/tomorrow*.	**For i dag/i morgen.** fohr ih·dahg/ih·**mawr**`·uhn

▶ For days, see page 166.

▶ For time, see page 165.

A *one-way [single]/ round-trip [return]* ticket.	**En enveisbillett/tur-returbillett.** ehn **ehn**´·vays·bihl·leht/tewr·reh·**tew**´r·bil·leht
A *first class/economy class* ticket.	**En billett på første klasse/ turistklasse.** ehn bihl·_leht_´ poh **furrs**`·tuh _klahs_`·suh/tew·_rihst_´·klahs·suh
How much?	**Hvor mye koster det?** voor _mui_`·uh _kohs_`·tuhr deh
Is there a discount for…?	**Er det noen rabatt for…?** ar deh _noo_`·uhn rah·_baht_´ fohr…
– children	**– barn** bahrn
– students	**– studenter** stew·_dehn_´·tuhr
– senior citizens	**– pensjonister** pahng·shoo·_nihs_´·tuhr
I have an e-ticket.	**Jeg har en e-billett.** yay hahr ehn **eh**´·bihl·leht
Can I buy a ticket on the *bus/train*?	**Kan man kjøpe billett på bussen/ toget?** kahn mahn khur`·puh bihl·_leht_´ poh **bews**·suhn/**taw**´·guh
I'd like to…my reservation.	**Jeg vil gjerne…reservasjonen.** yay vihl _ya_`r·nuh…reh·sehr·vah·_shoo_´n·uhn
– cancel	**– annullere** ahn·newl·_leh_´·ruh
– change	**– endre** _ehn_`·druh
– confirm	**– bekrefte** buh·_krehf_´·tuh

Plane

Getting to the Airport

How much is a taxi to the airport?	**Hva koster drosje til flyplassen?** vah <u>kohs`</u>·tuhr <u>drohsh`</u>·uh tihl <u>flui</u>´·plahs·suhn
To…Airport, please.	**Til…lufthavn.** tihl…<u>lewft</u>´·hahvn
My airline is…	**Jeg flyr med…** yay fluir meh…
My flight leaves at…	**Flyet mitt går…** <u>flui</u>´·uh miht gawr…

▶ For time, see page 165.

I'm in a hurry.	**Jeg har dårlig tid.** yay hahr <u>dawr</u>´·lih teed
Can you take an alternate route?	**Kan du kjøre en annen vei?** kahn dew <u>khur</u>`·ruh ehn <u>ahn</u>`·nuhn vay
Can you drive *faster/slower*?	**Kan du kjøre *fortere/saktere*?** kahn dew <u>khur</u>`·ruh <u>foor</u>`·tuh·ruh/<u>sahk</u>´·tuh·ruh

You May Hear…

Hvilket selskap flyr du med? <u>vihl</u>´·kuht sehl´·skahp fluir dew meh — What airline are you flying?

Innenlands eller utenlands? <u>ihn</u>`·nuhn·lahns <u>ehl</u>´·luhr <u>ew</u>`·tuhn·lahns — Domestic or international?

Hvilken terminal? <u>vihl</u>´·kuhn tehr·mih·<u>nahl</u>´ — What terminal?

Check-in and Boarding

Where's check-in?	**Hvor er innsjekkingsskranken?** voor ar <u>ihn</u>´·shehk·kihngs·skrahng·kuhn
My name is…	**Jeg heter…** yay <u>heh</u>´·tuhr…
I'm going to…	**Jeg skal til…** yay skahl tihl…
How much luggage is allowed?	**Hvor mye bagasje har man lov å ha med?** voor <u>mui</u>`·uh bah·<u>gah</u>´·shuh hahr mahn lawv oh hah meh

21

Can I have *a window/ an aisle* seat?	**Kan jeg få plass ved *vinduet/ midtgangen*?** kahn yay faw plahs veh <u>vihn</u>`·dew·uh/<u>miht</u>`·gahng·uhn
When do we *leave/ arrive*?	**Når *drar vi/kommer vi fram*?** nohr d*rahr* vee/<u>kohm</u>´·muhr *vee* frahm
Is the flight delayed?	**Er flyet forsinket?** ar <u>flui</u>´·uh fohr·<u>sihng</u>´·kuht
How late will it be?	**Hvor sent vil det bli?** voor s**eh**nt vihl deh bl**ee**

You May Hear…

Neste! <u>nehs</u>`·tuh	Next!
***Billetten/Passet*, takk.** bil·<u>leht</u>´·tuhn/ <u>pahs</u>´·suh tahk	Your *ticket/passport*, please.
Hvor mange kolli har du? voor <u>mang</u>`·uh <u>kohl</u>´·lih h**ah**r d**ew**	How many pieces of luggage do you have?
Du har for mye bagasje. d**ew** h**ah**r fohr <u>mui</u>`·uh bah·<u>gah</u>´·shuh	You have excess luggage.
Den er for *tung/stor* til håndbagasje. dehn ar fohr *tung/st**oo**r* tihl <u>hohn</u>`·bah·g**ah**·shuh	That's too *heavy/ large* for a carry-on [to carry on board].
Har du pakket disse *veskene/koffertene* selv? h**ah**r d**ew** <u>pahk</u>`·kuht <u>dihs</u>`·suh <u>vehs</u>`·kuh·nuh/<u>kuf</u>´·fuhr·tuh·nuh sehl	Did you pack these *bags/suitcases* yourself?
Tar du med noe for andre? t**ah**r d**ew** meh <u>noo</u>`·uh fohr <u>ahn</u>`·druh	Did anyone give you anything to carry?
Tøm lommene. turm <u>lum</u>`·muh·nuh	Empty your pockets.
Ta av deg skoene. t**ah** ah day <u>skoo</u>´·uh·nuh	Take off your shoes.
Avgang…er nå klar for ombordstigning. <u>ahv</u>`·gahng…ar n**aw** klahr fohr ohm·<u>boor</u>´·st**ee**g·nihng	Now boarding flight…

Luggage

Where *is/are*...?	**Hvor er...?** voor ar...
– the luggage carts [trolleys]	– **bagasjetrallene** bah·<u>gah</u>´·shuh·trahl·luh·nuh
– the luggage lockers	– **oppbevaringsboksene** <u>ohp</u>´·buh·**vah**·rihngs·bohk·suh·nuh
– the baggage claim	– **bagasjeutleveringen** bah·<u>gah</u>´·shuh·**ewt**·leh·veh·rihng·uhn
My suitcase was damaged.	**Kofferten min ble skadet.** <u>kuf</u>´·fuhr·tuhn mihn bleh <u>skah</u>`·duht

Finding Your Way

Where is...?	**Hvor er...?** voor ar...
– the currency exchange office	– **vekslingskontoret** <u>vehks</u>`·lihngs·kun·**too**·ruh
– the exit	– **utgangen** <u>ewt</u>`·gahng·uhn
– the taxi stand [rank]	– **drosjeholdeplassen** <u>drohsh</u>`·uh·hol·luh·plahs·suhn

▶ For directions, see page 32.

Train

How do I get to the train station?	**Hvordan kommer jeg til jernbanestasjonen?** <u>voor</u>´·dahn <u>kohm</u>´·muhr yay tihl <u>ya</u>´rn·bah·nuh·stah·shoo·nuhn
Is it far from here?	**Er det langt herfra?** ar deh lahngt <u>ha</u>´r·frah
Where *is/are*...?	**Hvor er...?** voor ar...
– the ticket office	– **billettluken** bihl·<u>leht</u>´·**lew**·kuhn
– the information desk	– **informasjonsskranken** ihn·fohr·mah·<u>shoo</u>´ns·skrahng·kuhn
– the tracks [platforms]	– **sporene** <u>spoo</u>´r·uh·nuh

▶ For directions, see page 32.

▶ For ticketing, see page 19.

Questions

Can I have a train schedule [timetable]?	**Kan jeg få en togtabell?** kahn yay faw ehn <u>tawg</u>·tah·behl
How long is the trip?	**Hvor lang er turen?** voor lang ar <u>tew</u>·ruhn
Do I have to change trains?	**Må jeg bytte tog?** maw yay <u>buit</u>·tuh tawg

Norway runs a train network more than 4,000 km (c. 2,500 miles) long, though the system is much more comprehensive in the south than the north. Oslo is the main hub for most long-distance, express and local trains. Long-distance lines that span the country are an excellent way to view the incredible Norwegian scenery.

A number of discounts are available. Children under 4 travel free of charge. Children under 16 and senior citizens travel at half price. Local buses, trams, subways and ferries run on an integrated network, so you may transfer at no additional cost. Keep in mind that buying a **flexikort** (multi-trip ticket) is cheaper than buying single tickets. For moving around the capital, you may also want to consider a 1-, 2- or 3-day (children's or family) **Oslo Pass**, which offers unlimited public transportation within greater Oslo and free entry to a number of museums and tourist attractions. For long-distance travel, you may consider a Eurorail (non-European residents), InterRail (European residents) or ScanRail (for travel within Scandinavia) pass.

Departures

Which track [platform] does the train to Skien leave from?	**Fra hvilket spor går toget til Skien?** frah <u>vihl'</u>·kuht spoor gawr <u>taw'</u>·guh til <u>sheh'</u>·uhn
Is this the track [platform] to…?	**Er dette sporet til…?** ar <u>deht'</u>·tuh <u>spoo'</u>·ruh tihl…
Where is track [platform]…?	**Hvor er spor…?** voor ar spoor…
Where do I change for…?	**Hvor må jeg bytte for å komme til…?** voor maw yay <u>buit'</u>·tuh fohr aw <u>kohm'</u>·muh tihl…

Boarding

Is this seat taken?	**Er denne plassen opptatt?** ar <u>dehn'</u>·nuh <u>plahs'</u>·suhn <u>ohp'</u>·taht
I think that's my seat.	**Jeg tror at det er min plass.** yay troor aht deh ar meen plahs

Ta plass. tah plahs	All aboard.
Billetter, takk. bihl-<u>leht</u>´-tuhr tahk	Tickets, please.
Du må bytte i... dew maw <u>buit</u>´-tuh ih...	You have to change at...
Neste holdeplass... <u>nehs</u>`-tuh <u>hohl</u>´-luh-plahs...	Next stop...

Bus and Train

Where's the bus station?	**Hvor er busstasjonen?** voor ar <u>bews</u>´-sta-sh**oo**-nuhn
How far is it?	**Hvor langt er det?** voor lahngt ar deh
How do I get to...?	**Hvordan kommer jeg til...?** <u>voor</u>´-dahn <u>kohm</u>´-muhr yay tihl...
Does the *bus/train* stop at (place/area)...?	**Stopper *bussen/trikken* (ved/på)...?** <u>stohp</u>´-puhr <u>bews</u>´-suhn/<u>trihk</u>´-kuhn (veh/poh)...
Can you tell me when to get off?	**Kan du si meg når jeg skal av?** kahn dew see may nohr yay skahl **ah**
Do I have to change buses?	**Må jeg bytte buss?** maw yay <u>buit</u>´-tuh bews
Can you stop here?	**Kan du stoppe her?** kahn dew <u>stohp</u>´-puh har

▶For ticketing, see page 19.

BUSSHOLDEPLASS/TRIKKEHOLDEPLASS	bus stop/train stop
INNGANG/UTGANG	enter/exit
STEMPLE BILLETTEN	stamp your ticket

Subway [Underground]

Where's the nearest subway [underground] station?	**Hvor er nærmeste T-banestasjon?** voor ar <u>nar</u>·mehs·tuh <u>teh</u>·bah·nuh·stah·sh<u>oo</u>n
Can I have a map of the subway [underground]?	**Kan jeg få et kart over T-banen?** kahn yay faw eht kart <u>**aw**</u>·vuhr <u>teh</u>·bah·nuh
Which line for…?	**Hvilken linje går til…?** <u>vihl</u>·kuhn <u>lihn</u>·yuh g<u>aw</u>r tihl…
Where do I change for…?	**Hvor må jeg bytte for å komme til…?** voor maw yay <u>buit</u>·tuh fohr aw <u>kohm</u>·muh tihl…
Is this the right train for…?	**Er dette toget til… ?** ar <u>deht</u>·tuh <u>taw</u>·guh tihl…
Where are we?	**Hvor er vi?** voor ar v<u>ee</u>

▶ For ticketing, see page 19.

The Oslo **Tunnelbane** or **T-bane** (subway) runs from approximately 5:30 a.m. to just after midnight. Buying a **flexikort** (multi-trip ticket) is a good idea if you plan on making numerous trips. It can be used to make transfers within one hour at no extra charge. An **Oslo Pass** is another discount travel pass, good for all forms of public transportation.

Boat and Ferry

When does the *boat/ferry* for…leave?	**Når går *båten/fergen* til…?** nohr g<u>aw</u>r <u>baw</u>·tuhn/<u>fehr</u>·guhn tihl…
Can I take my car?	**Kan jeg ta med bilen?** kahn yay <u>tah</u>·meh <u>bee</u>·luhn

▶ For ticketing, see page 19.

Ferry and boat travel is efficient in Norway. Most ferries and high-speed ships have frequent departure schedules, so you rarely have to wait in lines, and the cost for passenger and car transport is generally low. Besides regular ferry service, several companies offer cruises along the fjords. These are very popular during the summer months and tickets are more expensive during this period. Reservations should be made well in advance.

Bicycle and Motorcycle

I'd like to rent [hire]…	**Jeg vil gjerne leie…** yay vihl ya`r·nuh lay`·uh…
– a bicycle	**– en sykkel** ehn <u>suik</u>´·kuhl
– a moped	**– en moped** ehn mu·<u>peh</u>´d
– a motorcycle	**– en motorsykkel** ehn <u>moo</u>´·toor·suik·kuhl
How much per *day/ week*?	**Hvor mye koster det per *dag/uke*?** voor <u>mui</u>`·uh <u>kohs</u>`·tuhr deh pehr *dahg/<u>ew</u>`·kuh*
Can I have a *helmet/ lock*?	**Kan jeg få med *hjelm/lås*?** kahn yay <u>faw</u>`·meh *yehlm/<u>laws</u>*

If you enjoy cycling there are many well-planned routes throughout the country, through lush valleys and breathtaking fjords. Sign posts mark attractions along the way. You can bring your own bike or rent one easily. Considering the terrain, a **terrengsykkel** (mountain bike) is better than a racing bike.

Taxi

Where can I get a taxi?	**Hvor kan jeg få tak i en drosje?** voor kahn yay faw tahk ih ehn <u>droh</u>`·shuh
I'd like a taxi *now/for tomorrow* at…	**Jeg trenger en drosje *nå/i morgen klokken*…** yay <u>trehng</u>´·uhr ehn <u>droh</u>`·shuh *naw/ ih <u>mawr</u>`·uhn <u>klohk</u>´·kuhn*…

Can you pick me up…?	**Kan du hente meg…?** kahn dew <u>hehn`</u>·tuh may…
– at the airport	**– på flyplassen** poh <u>flui`</u>·plahs·suhn
– at the ferry landing	**– ved fergeleiet** veh <u>fer`</u>·guh·lay·uh
– at eight o'clock	**– klokken åtte** <u>klohk`</u>·kuhn <u>oht`</u>·tuh
Take me to…	**Kjør meg til…** khurr may tihl…
– this address	**– denne adressen** <u>dehn`</u>·nuh ahd·<u>rehs´</u>·suhn
– the airport	**– flyplassen** <u>flui`</u>·plahs·suhn
– the train station	**– jernbanestasjonen** <u>ya`rn</u>·bah·nuh·stah·shoon·uhn
I'm in a hurry.	**Jeg har dårlig tid.** yay hahr <u>dawr`</u>·lih teed
Can you drive *faster/ slower*?	**Kan du kjøre *fortere/saktere*?** kahn dew <u>khur`</u>·ruh <u>fohr´</u>·tuh·ruh/<u>sahk´</u>·tuh·ruh
Stop/Wait here.	***Stopp/Vent* her.** *stohp/vehnt* har
How much?	**Hvor mye koster det?** voor <u>mui`</u>·uh <u>kohs`</u>·tuhr deh
You said…crowns.	**Du sa…kroner.** dew sah…<u>kroo`</u>·nuhr
Can I have a receipt?	**Kan jeg få en kvittering?** kahn yay faw ehn kviht·<u>teh</u>´·rihng
Keep the change.	**Behold vekslepengene.** buh·<u>hohl´</u> <u>vehk`s</u>·luh·pehng·uh·nuh

You May Hear…

Hvor skal du? voor skahl dew	Where to?
Hva var adressen? vah vahr ahd·<u>rehs´</u>·suhn	What's the address?

i

Taxis can be hailed in the street, found at taxi stands or ordered by phone. All cabs are metered and service charges are included in the fare. You can tip the driver by rounding up the fare. Keep in mind that rates differ from place to place and travel by taxi is generally expensive. Ask for an approximate fare beforehand. Most taxis accept credit cards; however, if you're not carrying cash, be sure to double check first.

Car

Car Rental [Hire]

Where can I rent a car?	**Hvor kan jeg leie en bil?** voor kahn yay <u>lay</u>`·uh ehn b**eel**
I'd like to rent [hire]…	**Jeg vil gjerne leie…** yay vihl <u>ya</u>`r·nuh <u>lay</u>`·uh…
– a 2-/4-door car	– **en *to-dørs/firedørs* bil** ehn <u>*too*</u>`·durrs/ <u>*fee*</u>`·ruh-durrs b**eel**
– an automatic	– **en bil med automatgir** meh ev·tu·<u>mah</u>´t·geer
– a car with air conditioning	– **en bil med klimaanlegg** ehn b**eel** meh <u>klee</u>´·mah·ahn·lehg
– a car seat	– **et barnesete** eht <u>bahr</u>`·nuh·s**eh**·tuh
How much…?	**Hvor mye koster det…?** voor <u>muî</u>·uh <u>kohs</u>`·tuhr deh…
– per day	– **per dag** pehr d**ah**g
– per week	– **per uke** pehr <u>ew</u>`·kuh
– per kilometer	– **per kilometer** pehr <u>khee</u>´·lu·meh·tuhr
– for unlimited mileage	– **for ubegrenset kjørelengde** fohr <u>ew</u>`·buh·grehn·suht <u>khur</u>`·ruh·lehng·duh
– with insurance	– **inkludert forsikring** ihn·klew·<u>dehrt</u>´ fohr·<u>sihk</u>´·rihng
Are there any discounts?	**Er det noen rabatter?** ar deh <u>noo</u>`·uhn rah·<u>baht</u>´·tuhr

You May Hear...

Har du et internasjonalt førerkort? hahr dew eht <u>ihn</u>´·tuhr·nah·shu·<u>nahl</u>t <u>fur</u>´·ruhr·kohrt — Do you have an international driver's license?

Kan jeg få se passet? kahn yay faw seh <u>pahs</u>´·suh — Can I see your passport?

Vil du ha forsikring? vihl dew hah fohr·<u>sihk</u>´·rihng — Do you want insurance?

Det er et depositum på... deh ar eht deh·<u>poo</u>´·sih·tewm poh... — There is a deposit of...

Undertegn her. <u>ewn</u>`·nuhr·tayn har — Please sign here.

Gas [Petrol] Station

Where's the nearest gas [petrol] station?	**Hvor er nærmeste bensinstasjon?** voor ar <u>ner</u>´·mehs·tuh behn·<u>seen</u>´·stah·shoon
Fill it up, please.	**Full tank, takk.** fewl tahngk tahk
...liters, please.	**...liter bensin, takk.** ...<u>lee</u>´·tuhr behn·<u>seen</u>´ tahk
Can I pay *in cash/by credit card*?	**Kan jeg betale *kontant /med kredittkort*?** kahn yay buh·<u>tah</u>´·luh *kun·<u>tahn</u>´t / meh kreh·<u>diht</u>´·kohrt*

You May See...

NORMAL 95 OKTAN	regular
SUPER 98 OKTAN	premium [super]
DIESEL	diesel

Asking Directions

Are we on the right road for…?	**Er dette veien til…?** ar <u>deht</u>`-tuh <u>vay</u>´-uhn tih…
How far is it to…?	**Hvor langt er det til…?** voor lahngt ar deh tih…
Where's…?	**Hvor er…?** voor ar…
– …Street	**– …gate** …<u>gah</u>`-tuh
– this address	**– denne adressen** <u>dehn</u>`-nuh ahd-<u>rehs</u>´-suhn
– the highway [motorway]	**– motorveien** <u>moo</u>´-toor-vay-uhn
Can you show me where I am on the map?	**Kan du vise meg på kartet hvor jeg er?** kahn dew <u>vee</u>´-suh may paw <u>kahr</u>´-tuh voor yay ar
I'm lost.	**Jeg har gått meg vill.** yay hahr goht may vihl

You May Hear…

rett frem reht frehm	straight ahead
på venstre side poh <u>vehn</u>´-struh <u>see</u>`-duh	on the left
på høyre side poh <u>hury</u>´-ruh <u>see</u>`-duh	on the right
på/rundt hjørnet poh/rewnt <u>yurr</u>´-nuh	*on/around* the corner
midt imot… miht ih-<u>moot</u>´…	opposite…
bak… bahk…	behind…
ved siden av… veh <u>see</u>`-duhn ah…	next to…
etter… <u>eht</u>`-tuhr…	after…
nord/sør noor/surr	north/south
øst/vest urst/vehst	east/west
ved lyskrysset veh <u>luï`s</u>-kruis-suh	at the traffic light
ved veikrysset veh <u>vay</u>`-kruis-suh	at the intersection

You May See...

 STOPP   stop

 VIKEPLIKT   yield

 PARKERING FORBUDT   no parking

 ÉNVEISKJØRING   one way

 INNKJØRING FORBUDT   no entry

 FORBIKJØRING FORBUDT   no passing

 U-SVING FORBUDT   no U-turn

 GANGFELT   pedestrian crossing

Parking

Can I park here?	**Kan jeg parkere her?** kahn yay pahr·<u>keh´</u>·ruh har
Is there a parking lot [car park] nearby?	**Fins det en parkeringsplass i nærheten?** fins deh ehn pahr·<u>keh´</u>·rihngs·plahs ih <u>nar´</u>·heh·tuhn

How much…?	**Hvor mye koster det…?** voor <u>muî</u>·uh <u>kohs</u>`·tuhr deh…
– per hour	**– per time** pehr <u>tee</u>`·muh
– per day	**– per dag** pehr d<u>ah</u>g
– for overnight	**– over natten** <u>aw</u>´·vuhr <u>naht</u>´·tuhn

---

i Parking in Norway is restricted, particularly on weekdays. The most common system is the **P-automat** (automated parking meter). In this system, you park your car and then pay for an amount of time at the meter; the meter prints a ticket to be displayed on your dashboard. Another option is a **P-hus** (parking garage). When you enter the garage you receive a ticket. Before getting into your car to leave the garage, you must pay for your ticket at an automated machine or a manned booth.

Breakdown and Repairs

My car *broke down/ won't start.*	**Bilen *har fått motorstopp/starter ikke.*** <u>bee</u>´·luhn h*ah*r foht <u>moo</u>´·toor·stohp/ st<u>ah</u>r`·tuhr <u>ihk</u>`·kuh
Can you fix it?	**Kan du reparere den?** kahn d*ew* reh·pah·<u>reh</u>´·ruh dehn
When will it be ready?	**Når er den klar?** nohr *a*r dehn kl<u>ah</u>r
How much?	**Hvor mye koster det?** voor <u>muî</u>·uh <u>kohs</u>`·tuhr deh

Accidents

| There's been an accident. | **Det har skjedd en ulykke.** deh h*ah*r shehd ehn <u>ew</u>`·lui·kuh |
| Call *a doctor/an ambulance*! | **Ring etter *lege/sykebil*!** rihng <u>eht</u>`·tuhr <u>leh</u>´·guh/<u>sui</u>`·kuh·b*ee*l |

Essential

Can you recommend a hotel?	**Kan du anbefale et hotell?** kahn dew ahn´-buh-**fah**-luh eht hu-<u>tehl</u>´
I have a reservation.	**Jeg har bestilt rom.** yay hahr buh-<u>stihlt</u>´ rum
My name is…	**Jeg heter…** yay <u>heh</u>`-tuhr…
Do you have a room…?	**Har dere et rom…?** hahr <u>deh</u>`-ruh eht rum…
– for *én/to*	– **for** *én/to* fohr *ehn/too*
– with a bathroom	– **med bad** meh bahd
– with air conditioning	– **med klimaanlegg** meh <u>klee</u>´-mah-ahn-lehg
For tonight.	**For i natt.** fohr ih naht
For two nights.	**For to netter.** fohr too <u>neht</u>´-tuhr
For one week.	**For en uke.** fohr ehn <u>ew</u>`-kuh
How much?	**Hvor mye koster det?** voor <u>muï</u>`-uh <u>kohs</u>`-tuhr deh
Do you have anything cheaper?	**Har dere noe rimeligere?** hahr <u>deh</u>`-ruh <u>noo</u>`-uh <u>ree</u>`-muh-lih-uh-ruh
When's check-out?	**Når må jeg sjekke ut?** nohr maw yay <u>shehk</u>`-kuh ewt
Can I leave this in the safe?	**Kan jeg legge *denne/dette** igjen i safen?** kahn yay <u>lehg</u>`-guh *<u>dehn</u>`-nuh/ <u>deht</u>`-tuh* ih-<u>yehn</u>´ ih <u>sayf</u>´-uhn
Can I leave my bags?	**Kan jeg sette igjen bagasjen?** kahn yay <u>seht</u>`-tuh ih-<u>yehn</u>´ bah-<u>gah</u>´-shuhn

---

* For usage of **denne** and **dette**, see page 162.

Can I have *the bill/ a receipt*?	**Kan jeg få *regningen/en kvittering*?** kahn yay faw <u>ray</u>`·ning·uhn/ehn kviht·<u>teh</u>´·rihng
I'll pay *in cash/by credit card*.	**Jeg betaler *kontant/med kredittkort*.** yay buh·<u>tah</u>´·luhr kun·<u>tahnt</u>´/meh kreh·<u>diht</u>´·kohrt

If you didn't reserve a room before your arrival, the local tourist office can provide information and help you to arrange a reservation. The official website of the Norwegian Tourist Board, Visit Norway, can provide information about locations in particular cities.

▶For useful websites, see page 169.

Finding Lodging

Can you recommend a hotel?	**Kan du anbefale et hotell?** kahn dew <u>ahn</u>´·buh·<u>fah</u>·luh eht hu·<u>tehl</u>´
What is it near?	**Hva er det i nærheten?** vah ar deh ih <u>nar</u>´·heh·tuhn
How do I get there?	**Hvordan kommer jeg dit?** <u>voor</u>´·dahn <u>kohm</u>´·muhr yay d**ee**t

In Norway, there are a variety of accommodation alternatives in addition to more conventional options such as hotels, bed and breakfasts or **husrom** (rooms in private houses) and **vandrerhjem** (hostels). For a unique holiday experience you could consider a **bondegårdsferie** (farm stay), which lets you taste Norwegian farm life firsthand. Similarly, along the coast, you could arrange to stay in **rorbuer** (fisherman's cabins). **Hytter** (chalets or cabins) are available throughout the country as well.

At the Hotel

I have a reservation.	**Jeg har bestilt rom.** yay hahr buh·<u>stihlt</u>´ rum
My name is…	**Jeg heter…** yay <u>heh</u>`·tuhr…
Do you have a room…?	**Har dere et rom…?** hahr <u>deh</u>`·ruh eht rum…
– with a *bathroom/ shower*	– **med** *bad/dusj* meh *bahd/dewsh*
– with air conditioning	– **med klimaanlegg** meh <u>klee</u>´·mah·ahn·lehg
– that's *smoking/ non-smoking*	– **for** *røykere/ikke-røykere* fohr <u>ruryk</u>`·uh·ruh/<u>ihk</u>`·kuh·ruryk·uhr·uh
Does the hotel have…?	**Har hotellet…?** hahr hu·<u>tehl</u>´·uh…
– a computer	– **en datamaskin** ehn <u>dah</u>`·tah·mah·sheen
– an elevator [lift]	– **heis** hays
– room service	– **romservice** <u>rum</u>`·sur·vihs
– a gym	– **trimrom** <u>trihm</u>´·rum

Can I access the internet?	**Kan jeg bruke internett?** kahn yay br<u>ew</u>`·kuh <u>ihn</u>´·tuhr·neht
I need...	**Jeg trenger...** yay <u>trehng</u>´·uhr...
– an extra bed	**– en ekstra seng** ehn <u>ehks</u>´·trah sehng
– a cot [camp bed]	**– en feltseng** ehn <u>fehlt</u>´·sehng
– a crib [child's cot]	**– en barneseng** ehn <u>bahr</u>´·nuh·sehng

You May Hear...

Passet/kredittkortet **ditt, takk.** <u>pah</u>´·suh/ kreh·<u>diht</u>´·kohr·tuh diht tahk	Your *passport/credit card*, please.
Kan du fylle ut dette skjemaet? kahn dew f<u>ui</u>`·luh **ew**t <u>deht</u>´·tuh sh<u>eh</u>´·mah·uh	Can you fill out this form?
Undertegn her. <u>ewn</u>`·nuhr·tayn har	Sign here.

Price

| How much per *night/ week*? | **Hvor mye koster det per *natt/uke*?** voor m<u>ui</u>`·uh <u>kohs</u>`·tuhr deh pehr *naht/<u>ew</u>´·kuh* |
| Does the price include *breakfast/sales tax [VAT]*? | **Er *frokost/moms* inkludert i prisen?** ar <u>froo</u>´·kust/mums ihn·klu·<u>dehrt</u>´ ih <u>pree</u>´·suhn |

Questions

Where's...?	**Hvor er...?** voor ar...
– the bar	**– baren** <u>bah</u>´·ruhn
– the bathroom	**– toalettet** tu·ah·<u>leht</u>´·uh
– the elevator [lift]	**– heisen** <u>hay</u>´·suhn
Can I have...?	**Kan jeg få...?** kahn yay faw...
– a blanket	**– et ullteppe** eht <u>ewl</u>`·tehp·puh
– an iron	**– et strykejern** eht <u>strui</u>`·kuh·yarn

– a pillow	**– en pute** ehn <u>pew</u>`·tuh
– a soap	**– en såpe** ehn <u>saw</u>`·puh
– toilet paper	**– toalettpapir** tu·ah·<u>leht</u>´·pah·peer
– a towel	**– et håndkle** eht <u>hohng</u>`·kleh
Do you have an adapter for this?	**Har du en adapter til _denne/dette_*?** <u>ha</u>hr <u>d</u>ew ehn ahd·<u>ahp</u>´·tuhr tihl _<u>dehn</u>`·nuh/<u>deht</u>`·tuh_
How do I turn on the lights?	**Hvordan slår jeg på lyset?** <u>voor</u>´·dahn s<u>l</u>awr yay poh <u>lui</u>´s·uh
Can you wake me at…?	**Kan du vekke meg klokken…?** kahn d<u>e</u>w <u>vehk</u>`·kuh may <u>klohk</u>`·kuhn…
Could I have my things from the safe?	**Kan jeg få sakene mine fra safen?** kahn yay f<u>aw</u> <u>sah</u>`·kuh·nuh <u>mee</u>`·nuh frah <u>say</u>´·fuhn
Is/are there any _mail/ messages_ for me?	**Har det kommet _noe post/noen beskjed_ til meg?** hahr deh <u>kohm</u>`·muht _<u>noo</u>´·uh pohst/ <u>noo</u>´·uhn buh·<u>sheh</u>´ tihl_ may

Norwegian electricity is generally 220 volts and round two-pin plugs are typically used. British and American appliances may need an adapter.

You May See…

SKYV/TREKK	push/pull
TOALETT	restroom [toilet]
DUSJ	shower
HEIS	elevator [lift]

---

* For usage of **denne** and **dette**, see page 162.

TRAPP	stairs
VASKERI	laundry
IKKE FORSTYRR	do not disturb
BRANNDØR	fire door
NØDUTGANG	emergency/fire exit
VEKKING	wake-up call

Problems

There's a problem.	**Jeg har et problem.** yay hahr eht pru·<u>bleh</u>´m
I've lost my *key/key card*.	**Jeg har mistet *nøkkelen/nøkkelkortet*.** yay hahr <u>mihs</u>`·tuht *<u>nurk</u>`·kehl·uhn/<u>nurk</u>`·kehl·kor·tuh*
I've locked myself out of my room.	**Jeg har låst meg ute fra rommet.** yay hahr lawst may <u>ew</u>`·tuh fra <u>rum</u>´·muh
There's no *hot water/ toilet paper*.	**Jeg har ikke *varmt vann/toalettpapir*.** yay hahr <u>ihk</u>`·kuh *vahrmt vahn/tu·ah·<u>leht</u>´·pah·peer*
The room is dirty.	**Rommet er skittent** <u>rum</u>´·muh ar <u>shiht</u>`·tuhnt
There are bugs in our room.	**Det er insekter på rommet vårt.** deh ar <u>ihn</u>`·sehk·tuhr poh <u>rum</u>´·muh vohrt
…doesn't work.	**…virker ikke.** …<u>vihr</u>`·kuhr <u>ihk</u>`·kuh
Can you fix…?	**Kan du få fikset…?** kahn dew faw <u>fihk</u>`·suht…
– the air conditioning	– **klimaanlegget** <u>klee</u>´·mah·ahn·lehg·guh
– the fan	– **viften** <u>vihf</u>`·tuhn
– the heat [heating]	– **varmen** <u>vahr</u>`·muhn
– the light	– **lyset** <u>lui</u>´s·uh
– the TV	– **TVen** <u>teh</u>`·veh·uhn
– the toilet	– **toalettet** tu·ah·<u>leht</u>´·tuh
I'd like to move to another room.	**Jeg vil gjerne flytte til et annet rom.** yay vihl <u>ya</u>`r·nuh <u>fluit</u>`·tuh tihl eht <u>ahn</u>`·nuht rum

Check-out

When's check-out?	**Når må jeg sjekke ut?** nohr maw yay <u>shehk</u>´·kuh ewt
Could I leave my bags here until…?	**Kan jeg sette igjen bagasjen min til…?** kahn yay <u>seht</u>´·tuh ih·<u>yehn</u>´ bah·<u>gah</u>´·shuhn mihn tihl…
Can I have *an itemized bill/ a receipt*?	**Kan jeg få en *spesifisert regning/ kvittering*?** kahn yay faw ehn *speh·sih·fih·<u>sehrt</u>´ <u>ray</u>´·ning/kviht·<u>teh</u>´·rihng*
I think there's a mistake in the bill.	**Jeg tror det er en feil på regningen.** yay <u>troo</u>r deh ar ehn fayl poh <u>ray</u>´·ning·uhn
I'll pay *in cash/by credit card*.	**Jeg betaler *kontant/med kredittkort*.** yay buh·<u>tah</u>´·luhr *kun·<u>tahnt</u>´/meh kreh·<u>diht</u>´·kohrt*

Renting ———————————————

I've reserved *an apartment/a room*.	**Jeg har bestilt *leilighet/rom*.** yay hahr buh·<u>stihlt</u>´ *<u>lay</u>`·li·<u>heht</u>/rum*
My name is…	**Jeg heter…** yay <u>heh</u>`·tuhr…
Can I have the *key/ key card*?	**Kan jeg få *nøkkelen/nøkkelkortet*?** kahn yay faw *<u>nurk</u>`·kuhl·uhn/ <u>nurk</u>`·kuhl·kor·tuh*
Are there…?	**Fins det…?** fihns deh…
– dishes	– **servise** sehr·<u>vee</u>´·suh
– pillows	– **puter** <u>pew</u>`·tuhr
– sheets	– **lakener** <u>lah</u>´·kuhn·uhr
– towels	– **håndklær** <u>hohng</u>`·klar
When/Where do I put out the trash [rubbish]?	***Når/Hvor* setter jeg ut søppelet?** *nohr/voor* <u>seht</u>´·tuhr yay **ew**t <u>surp</u>´·puhl·uh
…is broken.	**…er gått i stykker.** …ar goht ih <u>stuik</u>´·kuhr

How does…work?	Hvordan virker…? <u>voor´</u>·dahn <u>vihr`</u>·kuhr
– the air conditioner	– klimaanlegget <u>klee´</u>·mah·ahn·lehg·guh
– the dishwasher	– oppvaskmaskinen <u>ohp`</u>·vahsk·mah·sh**ee**n·uhn
– the freezer	– fryseren <u>frui`</u>·suhr·uhn
– the heater	– varmeovnen <u>vahr`</u>·muh·ohv·nuhn
– the microwave	– mikrobølgeovnen <u>mih´</u>·kru·burl·guh·ohv·nuhn
– the refrigerator	– kjøleskapet <u>khur`</u>·luh·skahpuh
– the stove	– komfyren kohm·<u>fui`</u>·ruhn
– the washing machine	– vaskemaskinen <u>vahs`</u>·kuh·mah·sh**ee**n·uhn

Household Items

I need…	Jeg trenger… yay <u>trehng´</u>·uhr…
– an adapter	– en adapter ehn ah·<u>dahp´</u>·tuhr
– aluminum [kitchen] foil	– aluminiumsfolie ah·lew·<u>**meen**´</u>·yewms·**fool**·yuh
– a bottle opener	– en flaskeåpner ehn <u>flahs`</u>·kuh·awp·nuhr
– a broom	– en feiekost ehn <u>fay`</u>·uh·kust
– a can opener	– en boksåpner ehn <u>bohks`</u>·awp·nuhr
– cleaning supplies	– rengjøringsmidler <u>rehn`</u>·yurr·ihngs·mihd·luhr
– a corkscrew	– en korketrekker ehn <u>kohr`</u>·kuh·trehk·kuhr
– detergent	– vaskemiddel <u>vahs`</u>·kuh·mihd·duhl
– dish detergent	– oppvaskmiddel <u>ohp`</u>·vahsk·mid·duhl
– garbage [rubbish] bags	– søppelsekker <u>surp`</u>·puhl·sehk·kuhr
– a light bulb	– en lyspære ehn <u>lui`s</u>·pa·ruh
– matches	– fyrstikker <u>fuir`</u>·stihk·kuhr

– a napkin	– **en serviett** ehn sehrv·<u>yeht</u>´
– paper towels	– **husholdningspapir** hews·<u>hohl</u>´·nihngs·pah·p**ee**r
– plastic wrap [cling film]	– **plastfolie** <u>plahst</u>´·**fool**·yuh
– a plunger	– **en klosettpumpe** ehn klu·<u>seht</u>´·pum·puh
– scissors	– **en saks** ehn sahks
– a vacuum cleaner	– **en støvsuger** ehn <u>stur</u>´v·**sewg**·uhr

▶ For dishes and utensils, see page 61.

▶ For oven temperatures, see page 169.

Hostel

Do you have any places left for tonight?	**Har dere noen plasser ledig for i natt?** h**a**hr <u>deh</u>`·ruh <u>noo</u>`·uhn <u>plahs</u>`·suhr <u>leh</u>`·dih fohr ih naht
Can I have…?	**Kan jeg få…?** kahn yay f**aw**…
– a *single/double* room	– **et *enkeltrom/dobbeltrom*** eht <u>ehng</u>´·kuhlt·rum/<u>dohb</u>´·buhlt·rum
– a blanket	– **et ullteppe** eht <u>ewl</u>`·tehp·puh
– a pillow	– **en pute** ehn <u>pew</u>`·tuh
– soap	– **såpe** <u>saw</u>`·puh
– towels	– **håndklær** <u>hohng</u>`·kl**a**r
What time do you lock up?	**Når stenges ytterdøra?** nohr <u>stehng</u>`·uhs <u>uit</u>`·tuhr·d**ur**·rah

There are well over 100 hostels throughout Norway run by two different chains: Hostelling International, monitored by **Norske Vandrerhjem** (the Norwegian branch of Hostelling International), and VIP Backpackers Resorts International. Located in cities as well as natural settings like fjords and along the coast, hostels are an inexpensive accommodation option. In many cases you may request a private or shared room. The charge per night covers only the cost of the room. Linens may be brought from home or rented. Meals are separate.

Camping

Can we camp here?	**Kan vi campe her?**	kahn vee <u>kehm</u>`·puh har
Is there a camp site nearby?	**Er det en campingplass i nærheten?**	ar deh ehn <u>kehm</u>´·pihng·plahs ih <u>nar</u>´·heh·tuhn
What is the charge per *day/week*?	**Hva koster det per *dag/uke*?**	vah <u>kohs</u>`·tuhr deh pehr *dahg/<u>ew</u>`·kuh*
Are there…?	**Fins det…?**	fihns deh…
– cooking facilities	**– kokemuligheter**	<u>koo</u>`·kuh·m**ew**·lih·heht·uhr
– electrical outlets	**– innlagt strøm**	<u>ihn</u>´·lahkt strurm
– laundry facilities	**– vaskemuligheter**	<u>vahs</u>`·kuh·m**ew**·lih·heht·uhr
– showers	**– dusj**	dewsh
– tents for rent [hire]	**– telt til leie**	tehlt tihl <u>lay</u>`·uh
Where can I empty the chemical toilet?	**Hvor kan jeg tømme det kjemiske toalettet?**	voor kahn yay <u>turm</u>`·muh de <u>kh**eh**</u>´·mihs·kuh tu·ah·<u>leht</u>´·uh

You May See…

DRIKKEVANN	drinking water
CAMPING FORBUDT	no camping
BRUK AV ÅPEN ILD FORBUDT	no fires
GRILLING FORBUDT	no barbecues

▶For household items, see page 42.

▶For dishes, utensils and kitchen tools, see page 61.

Essential

Where's an internet cafe?	**Hvor finner jeg en internettkafé?** voor fihn´·nuhr yay ehn ihn´·tuhr·neht·kah·**f**eh
Can I access *the internet/check e-mail*?	**Kan jeg *bruke internett/sjekke e-post*?** kahn yay <u>brew`·kuh</u> <u>ihn´·tuhr·neht/ shehk`·kuh</u> **eh´**·pohst
How much per *hour/half hour*?	**Hvor mye er det for en *time/halv time*?** voor <u>mui`</u>·uh ar deh fohr ehn <u>tee`</u>·muh/ hahl <u>tee`</u>·muh
How do I *connect/log on*?	**Hvordan *kobler jeg meg opp/logger jeg meg inn*?** <u>voor`</u>·dahn <u>kohb`</u>·luhr yay may ohp/<u>lohg`</u>·guhr yay may ihn
Can I have a phone card?	**Kan jeg få et telefonkort?** kahn yay f**aw** eht teh·luh·**foon**´·kohrt
Can I have your phone number?	**Kan jeg få telefonnummeret ditt?** kahn yay f**aw** teh·luh·**foon**´·num·muhr·uh diht
Here's my *number/e-mail address*.	**Her har du *nummeret mitt/e-postadressen min*.** har hahr dew <u>num´</u>·muhr·uh miht/**eh**´·pohst·ahd·rehs·suhn mihn
Call me.	**Ring meg.** rihng may
E-mail me.	**Send meg en e-post.** sehn may ehn **eh**´·pohst
Hello. This is…	**Hallo. Dette er…** hah·<u>loo</u>´ <u>deht</u>´·tuh ar…
I'd like to speak to…	**Kan jeg få snakke med…?** kahn yay f**aw** <u>snahk</u>´·kuh meh…
Can you repeat that?	**Kan du gjenta det?** kahn d**ew** <u>yehn</u>´·tah deh
I'll call back later.	**Jeg ringer igjen senere.** yay <u>rihng</u>`·uhr ih·<u>yehn</u>´ <u>seh</u>`·nuh·ruh

Goodbye.	**Adjø.** ahd·<u>yur</u>´
Where's the post office?	**Hvor er postkontoret?** voor ar <u>pohst</u>´·kun·toor·uh
Can I send this to…?	**Kan jeg få sendt dette til…?** kahn yay faw sehnt <u>deht</u>`·tuh tihl…

Computer, Internet and E-mail

Where's an internet cafe?	**Hvor finner jeg en internettkafé?** voor <u>fihn</u>´·nuhr yay ehn <u>ihn</u>´·tuhr·neht·kah·feh
Does it have wireless internet?	**Har den trådløst internett?** <u>hah</u>r dehn <u>traw</u>`·lurst <u>ihn</u>´·tuhr·neht
How do I turn the computer *on/off*?	**Hvordan slår jeg *på/av* datamaskinen?** <u>voor</u>´·dahn slawr yay *paw/ah* <u>dah</u>´·tah·mah·sheen·uhn
Can I…?	**Kan jeg…?** kahn yay…
– access the Internet	– **bruke internett** <u>brew</u>`·kuh <u>ihn</u>´·tuhr·neht
– check e-mail	– **sjekke e-post** <u>shehk</u>`·kuh <u>eh</u>´·pohst
– print	– **skrive ut** <u>skree</u>`·vuh ewt
How much per *hour/ half hour*?	**Hvor mye er det for en *time/halv time*?** voor <u>mui</u>`·uh ar deh fohr ehn <u>tee</u>`·muh/ hahl <u>tee</u>`·muh
How do I…?	**Hvordan…?** <u>voor</u>´·dahn…
– connect/disconnect	– **kobler jeg meg *opp/fra*** <u>kohb</u>`·luhr yay may *ohp/frah*
– log *on/off*	– **logger jeg meg *inn/ut*** <u>lohg</u>`·guhr jay may ihn/*ewt*
– type this symbol	– **skriver jeg dette tegnet** <u>skree</u>´·vuhr yay <u>deht</u>`·tuh <u>tay</u>´·nuh
What's your e-mail?	**Hva er e-postadressen din?** vah ar <u>eh</u>´·pohst·ahd·rehs·suhn dihn

My e-mail is…	**E-postadressen min er…** <u>eh</u>´·pohst·ahd·rehs·suhn mihn ar…

Phone

Can I have a *phone card/prepaid calling time for… crowns*?	**Kan jeg få et *telefonkort/ringetid for… kroner*?** kahn yay faw eht teh·luh·<u>foon</u>´·kohrt/ <u>rihng</u>`·uh·**teed** fohr…<u>kroo</u>`n·uhr
How much?	**Hvor mye koster det?** voor <u>mui</u>`·uh <u>kohs</u>`·tuhr deh
My cell [mobile] phone doesn't work here.	**Mobilen min virker ikke her.** mu·<u>beel</u>´·uhn mihn <u>vihr</u>`·kuhr <u>ihk</u>`·kuh har
What's the *area/ country* code for…?	**Hva er *retningsnummeret/landkoden* til…?** vah ar <u>reht</u>`·nihngs·num·muhr·uh/ <u>lahn</u>`·**kood**·uhn tihl…
What's the number for Information?	**Hva er nummeret til Opplysningen?** vah ar <u>num</u>´·muhr·uh tihl ohp·<u>luis</u>´·nihng·uhn

Can I have the number for…?	**Kan jeg få nummeret til…?** kahn yay faw <u>num´</u>·muhr·uh tihl…
Can I have your number?	**Kan jeg få nummeret ditt?** kahn yay faw <u>num´</u>·muhr·uh diht
My number is…	**Nummeret mitt er…** <u>num´</u>·muhr·uh miht ar…

▶ For numbers, see page 163.

Can you call me?	**Kan du ringe meg?** kahn dew <u>rihng`</u>·uh may
Can you text me?	**Kan du sende meg en tekstmelding?** kahn dew <u>sehn`</u>·nuh may ehn <u>tehkst´</u>·mehl·lihng
I'll call you.	**Jeg ringer deg.** yay <u>rihng`</u>·uhr day
I'll text you.	**Jeg sender deg en tekstmelding.** yay <u>sehn`</u>·nuhr day ehn <u>tehkst´</u>·mehl·lihng

On the Phone

Hello. This is…	**Hallo. Dette er…** hah·<u>loo´</u> <u>deht`</u>·tuh ar…
Can I speak to…?	**Kan jeg få snakke med…?** kahn yay faw <u>snahk`</u>·kuh meh…
Extension…	**Linje…** <u>lihn`</u>·yuh…
Can you speak *louder/ more slowly*?	**Kan du snakke litt *høyere/ langsommere*?** kahn dew <u>snahk`</u>·kuh liht <u>*hury`*</u>·uhr·uh/<u>*lahng`*</u>·sohm·muhr·uh
Can you repeat that?	**Kan du gjenta det?** kahn dew <u>yehn´</u>·tah deh
I'll call back later.	**Jeg ringer igjen senere.** yay <u>rihng`</u>·uhr ih·<u>yehn´</u> <u>seh`</u>·nuh·ruh
Goodbye.	**Adjø.** ahd·<u>yur´</u>

▶ For business travel, see page 140.

You May Hear...

Hvem er det som ringer? vehm ar deh sohm <u>rihng</u>`·uhr	Who's calling?
Et øyeblikk. eht <u>ury</u>`·uh·blihk	Hold on.
Jeg skal sette deg over. yay skahl <u>seht</u>`·tuh day <u>aw</u>´·vuhr	I'll put you through.
Han/Hun **er ute for øyeblikket.** *hahn/hewn* ar <u>ew</u>`·tuh fohr <u>ury</u>`·uh·blihk·kuh	*He's/She's* out at the moment.
Han/Hun **kan ikke ta telefonen akkurat nå.** *hahn/hewn* kahn <u>ihk</u>`·kuh tah teh·luh·<u>foon</u>´·uhn <u>ahk</u>´·kew·raht n**aw**	*He/She* can't come to the phone right now.
Vil du legge igjen en beskjed? vihl dew <u>lehg</u>`·guh ih·<u>yehn</u>´ ehn buh·<u>sheh</u>´	Would you like to leave a message?
Ring igjen *senere/om ti minutter.* rihng ih·<u>yehn</u>´ <u>seh</u>`·nuh·ruh/ohm tee mihn·<u>ewt</u>´·tuhr	Call back *later/in 10 minutes.*
Kan *han/hun* **ringe deg opp?** kahn *hahn/hewn* <u>rihng</u>`·uh day ohp	Can *he/she* call you back?
Hva er nummeret ditt? v**ah** ar <u>num</u>´·muh·ruh diht	What's your number?

In Norway, public phones accept coins, credit cards or **telekort** (prepaid phone cards), which are available at most kiosks, post offices and major train stations.
Important telephone numbers:
Emergencies: Fire 110, Police 112, Medical Emergencies 113
Information, 1880
Operator Assistance, 1882

To call the U.S. or Canada from Norway, dial 00 + 1 + area code + phone number. To call the U.K., dial 00 + 44 + area code (minus the first 0) + phone number.

Fax

Can I *send/receive* a fax here?	**Kan jeg *sende/motta* faks her?** kahn yay _sehn'_·nuh/_**moot**'_·tah fahks har
What's the fax number?	**Hva er faksnummeret?** vah ar _fahks'_·num·muh·ruh
Please fax this to…	**Kan du fakse dette til…** kahn dew _fahks'_·uh _deht'_·tuh tihl…

Post Office

Where's the *post office/mailbox [postbox]*?	**Hvor finner jeg *et postkontor/en postkasse*?** voor _fihn'_·nuhr yay _eht pohst'_·kun·**too**r/ehn _pohst'_·kahs·suh
A stamp for this *letter/postcard*, please.	**Et frimerke til dette *brevet/kortet*, takk.** eht _free'_·mehrk·uh til _deht'_·tuh _breh'_·vuh/_kohr'_·tuh tahk
How much?	**Hvor mye koster det?** voor _mui'_·uh _kohs'_·tuhr deh
I'd like to send this by *airmail/express mail*.	**Jeg vil gjerne sende dette med *flypost/ekspress*.** yay vihl _ya`r_·nuh _sehn'_·nuh _deht'_·tuh meh _flui·**pohst**/ehks·**prehs**'_
Can I have a receipt?	**Kan jeg få kvittering?** kahn yay faw kviht·_teh'_·rihng

50

You May Hear...

Kan du fylle ut en tolldeklarasjon? kahn dew <u>fuil</u>`·luh **ew**t ehn <u>tohl</u>`·deh·klah·rah·sh**oo**n

Can you fill out the customs declaration form?

Hva er verdien? v**ah** **a**r vehr·<u>dee</u>´·uhn

What's the value?

Hva er det inni? v**ah** **a**r deh <u>ihn</u>`·ih

What's inside?

Norwegian post offices are generally open Monday to Friday from 8 a.m. to 4 p.m. and Saturday from 9 a.m. to 1 p.m. Mailboxes are painted red and display the trumpet symbol of the post office.

▼ Food

▶ **Eating Out**   *53*

▶ **Meals**   *62*

▶ **Drinks**   *79*

▶ **Menu Reader**   *83*

Essential

Can you recommend a good *restaurant/bar*?	**Kan du anbefale en bra *restaurant/bar*?** kahn dew <u>ahn</u>´·buh·**fah**·luh ehn brah rehs·tew·<u>rahng</u>´/b**ah**r
Is there *a traditional Norwegian/an inexpensive* restaurant near here?	**Fins det en *typisk norsk/billig* restaurant i nærheten?** fihns deh ehn <u>tui</u>´·pihsk nohrsk/<u>bihl</u>´·lih rehs·tew·**rahng**´ ih <u>nar</u>´·heh·tuhn
A table for…	**Et bord til…** eht b**oo**r tihl…
Could we have a table *here/there*?	**Kan vi få et bord *her/der*?** kahn vee faw eht eht b**oo**r h**a**r/d**a**r
Could we have a table in the corner?	**Kan vi få et hjørnebord?** kahn vee faw eht eht **yur**`n·uh·b**oo**r
I'm waiting for someone.	**Jeg venter på noen.** yay <u>vehn</u>`·tuhr poh <u>noo</u>`·uhn
Where is the restroom [toilet]?	**Hvor er toalettet?** v**oo**r **a**r tu·ah·<u>leht</u>´·tuh
Can I have a menu?	**Kan jeg få se menyen?** kahn yay faw seh meh·<u>nui</u>´·uhn
What do you recommend?	**Hva kan du anbefale?** vah kahn dew <u>ahn</u>´·buh·**fah**·luh
I'd like…	**Jeg vil gjerne ha…** yay vihl <u>ya</u>`r·nuh hah…
Can I have more…?	**Kan jeg få litt mer…?** kahn yay faw liht mehr…
Enjoy your meal!	**God appetitt!** gu ahp·puh·<u>tiht</u>´
Can I have the check [bill]?	**Kan jeg få regningen?** kahn yay faw <u>ray</u>`·nihng·uhn

Is service included?	**Er service inkludert?** ar surr´·vihs ing·klew·**dehrt´**
Can I pay by credit card?	**Kan jeg betale med kredittkort?** kahn yay buh·**tah´**·luh meh kreh·**diht´**·kohrt
Can I have a receipt?	**Kan jeg få kvittering?** kahn yay faw kviht·**teh´**·rihng
Thank you.	**Takk.** tahk

Restaurant Types

Can you recommend…?	**Kan du anbefale…?** kahn dew **ahn´**·buh·**fah**·luh…
– a restaurant	**– en restaurant** ehn rehs·tew·**rahng´**
– a bar	**– en bar** ehn ba**h**r
– a café	**– en kafé** ehn kah·**feh´**
– a fast-food place	**– en hurtigmatrestaurant** ehn **hewr**`·tih·maht·rehs·tew·rahng

Reservations and Questions

I'd like to reserve a table…	**Jeg vil gjerne bestille et bord…** yay vihl **ya**`r·nuh buhs·**tihl´**·luh eht boor…
– for four	**– til fire** tihl **fee**`·ruh
– for this evening	**– til i kveld** tihl ih kvehl
– for tomorrow at…	**– til i morgen klokken…** tihl ih **maw**`·ruhn **klohk**`·kuhn…

▶ For time, see page 165.

A table for two, please.	**Et bord til to, takk.** eht boor´ tihl too tahk
We have a reservation.	**Vi har bestilt bord.** vee ha**h**r buhs·**tihlt´** boor
My name is…	**Jeg heter…** yay **heh**`·tuhr…

54

Could we have…?	**Kan vi få et…?** kahn vee faw…
– a table *here/there*	– **et bord *her/der*** eht boor *har/dar*
– a table in the corner	– **et hjørnebord** eht <u>yur</u>`·nuh·boor
– a table by the window	– **vindusbord** <u>vihn</u>`·dews·boor
Where is the restroom [toilet]?	**Hvor er toalettet?** voor ar tu·ah·<u>leht</u>´·tuh

You May Hear…

Har dere bestilt bord? hahr <u>deh</u>·ruh buhs·<u>tihlt</u>´ boor	Do you have a reservation?
Er dere klare til å bestille? ar <u>deh</u>·ruh <u>klah</u>´·ruh tihl aw buhs·<u>tihl</u>´·luh	Are you ready to order?
Hva skal det være? vah skahl deh <u>va</u>`·ruh	What would you like?
God appetitt. gu ahp·puh·<u>tiht</u>´	Enjoy your meal.

Ordering

Waiter/Waitress!	**Servitør!** ser·vih·<u>turr</u>´
We're ready to order.	**Vi er klare til å bestille.** vee ar <u>klah</u>`·ruh tihl aw buhs·<u>tihl</u>´·luh
Can I have the wine list?	**Kan jeg få se vinkartet?** kahn yay faw seh <u>veen</u>`·kahr·tuh
I'd like…	**Jeg vil gjerne ha…** yay vihl <u>ya</u>`r·nuh hah…
– a bottle of…	**– en flaske…** ehn <u>flahs</u>`·kuh…
– a carafe of…	**– en karaffel…** ehn kah·<u>rahf</u>´·fuhl…
– a glass of…	**– et glass…** eht glahs…

▶ For alcoholic and non-alcoholic drinks, see page 79.

Can I have a menu?	**Kan jeg få se menyen?** kahn yay faw seh meh·<u>nui</u>´·uhn
Do you have…?	**Har dere…?** hahr deh`·ruh…
– a menu in English	**– en meny på engelsk** ehn meh·<u>nui</u>´ poh <u>ehng</u>´·ehlsk
– a set menu	**– en fast meny** ehn fahst meh·<u>nui</u>´
– a children's menu	**– en barnemeny** ehn <u>bahr</u>`·nuh·meh·nui
What do you recommend?	**Hva kan du anbefale?** vah kahn dew <u>ahn</u>´·buh·**fah**·luh
What's this?	**Hva er dette?** vah ar <u>deht</u>`·tuh
What's in it?	**Hva inneholder *den/det**?** vah <u>ihn</u>`·nuh·hawl·luhr *dehn/deh*
Is it spicy?	**Er *den/det** sterkt krydret?** ar *dehn/deh* sterkt <u>kruid</u>`·ruht
It's to go [take away].	**Jeg tar det med meg.** yay tahr´ deh meh may

* For usage of **den** and **det**, see page 160.

56

You May See...

INNGANGSPENGER	cover charge
DAGENS MENY	menu of the day
SPESIALITETER	specials

Cooking Methods

baked	**bakt** bahkt
boiled	**kokt** kukt
braised	**braisert** brahs·seh´rt
breaded	**panert** pah·neh´rt
creamed	**fløtegratinert** flur`·tuh·grah·tih·nehrt
diced	**i terninger** ih ter`·nihng·uhr
fried	**stekt** stehkt
grilled (broiled)	**grillet** grihl`·luht
poached	**pochert** pu·sheh´rt
roasted	**ovnsstekt** ohvns`·stehkt
sautéed	**sautert** soh·teh´rt
smoked	**røkt** rurkt
steamed	**dampet** dahm`·puht
stewed	**stuet** stew`·uht
stuffed	**fylt** fuilt

Special Requirements

I'm...	**Jeg er...** yay ar...
– a diabetic	– **diabetiker** dih·ah·beh´·tihk·uhr
– lactose intolerant	– **laktoseintolerant** lahk·too`·suh·ihn·toh·luh·rahnt
– a vegetarian	– **vegetarianer** veh·guh·tahr·ih·ah´·nuhr

I'm allergic to...	**Jeg er allergisk mot...** yay ar ah·<u>lehr´</u>·gihsk m**oo**t...
I can't eat...	**Jeg kan ikke spise...** yay kahn <u>ihk`</u>·kuh <u>sp**ee**´</u>·suh...
– dairy	**– melkeprodukter** <u>mehl´</u>·kuh·pru·dewk·tuhr
– gluten	**– gluten** <u>glew´</u>·tuhn
– nuts	**– nøtter** <u>nurt´</u>·tuhr
– pork	**– svinekjøtt** <u>svee</u>`·nuh·khurt
– shellfish	**– skalldyr** <u>skahl´</u>·duir
– spicy foods	**– sterkt krydret mat** sterkt <u>kruid´</u>·ruht m**ah**t
– wheat	**– hvete** <u>veh`</u>·tuh
Is it *halal/kosher*?	**Er maten *halal/kosher*?** ar <u>mah´</u>·tuhn hahl·<u>ahl´</u>/<u>kohsh´</u>·uhr

Dining with Kids

Do you have children's portions?	**Har dere barneporsjoner?** hahr d<u>eh`</u>·ruh <u>bahr`</u>·nuh·poor·shoon·uhr
Can I have a *highchair/child's seat*?	**Kan jeg få en *babystol/barnestol*?** kahn yay faw ehn <u>beh´</u>·bih·stool/<u>bahr`</u>·nuh·stool
Where can I *feed/change* the baby?	**Hvor kan jeg *amme/bytte* på babyen?** voor kahn yay <u>ah`</u>·muh/<u>buit´</u>·tuh poh <u>beh`</u>·bih·uhn
Can you warm this?	**Kan du varme opp denne?** kahn d**e**w <u>vahr`</u>·muh ohp <u>dehn`</u>·nuh

▶ For travel with children, see page 142.

Complaints

| How much longer will our food be? | **Hvor lenge drøyer det med maten?** vur <u>lehng`</u>·uh <u>drury´</u>·uhr deh meh <u>maht´</u>·uhn |
| We can't wait any longer. | **Vi kan ikke vente lenger.** vee kahn <u>ihk`</u>·kuh <u>vehn`</u>·tuh <u>lehng`</u>·uhr |

We're leaving.	**Vi drar.** vee drahr
That's not what I ordered.	**Dette er ikke det jeg bestilte.** <u>deht</u>`·tuh ar <u>ihk</u>`·kuh deh yay buh·<u>stihl</u>`·tuh
I asked for…	**Jeg ba om…** yay bah um…
I can't eat this.	**Jeg kan ikke spise dette.** yay kahn <u>ihk</u>`·kuh <u>spee</u>`·suh <u>deht</u>`·tuh
This is too…	**Det er for…** deh ar fohr…
– cold/hot	**– kaldt/varmt** kahlt/varmt
– salty/spicy	**– salt/krydret** sahlt/<u>kruid</u>`·ruht
– tough/bland	**– seigt/mildt** saykt/mihlt
This isn't *clean/fresh*.	**Dette er ikke *rent/ferskt*.** <u>deht</u>`·tuh ar <u>ihk</u>`·kuh *rehnt/ferskt*

Paying

Can I have the check [bill]?	**Kan jeg får regningen?** kahn yay faw <u>rayn</u>`·nihng·uhn
We'd like to pay separately.	**Vi vil gjerne betale hver for oss.** vee vihl yar`·nuh buh·<u>tah</u>`·luh var fohr ohs
It's all together.	**Det er for alt sammen.** deh ar fohr ahlt <u>sam</u>·muhn
Is service included?	**Er service inkludert?** ar <u>surr</u>`·vihs ihng·klew·<u>dehrt</u>´
What's this amout for?	**Hva står dette beløpet for?** vah stawr <u>deht</u>`·tuh buh·<u>lur</u>`·puh fohr
I didn't have that. I had…	**Jeg spiste ikke det. Jeg spiste…** yay <u>spihs</u>`·tuh <u>ihk</u>`·kuh deh yay <u>spihs</u>`·tuh…
Can I pay by credit card?	**Kan jeg betale med kredittkort?** kahn yay buh·<u>tah</u>´·luh meh kreh·<u>diht</u>´·kort

Can I have an itemized bill/a receipt?	**Kan jeg få en spesifisert regning/ en kvittering?** kahn yay faw ehn speh·sih·fih·**seh´rt** ray´·nihng/ehn kviht·**teh´**·rihng
That was a very good meal.	**Maten smakte veldig godt.** maht´·uhn smahk`·tuh vehl`·dih goht

A 10-15% service charge is typically included in most restaurant bills. Wait staff, however, often receives an extra 5-10% tip.

Market

Where are the carts [trolleys]/baskets?	**Hvor er handlevognene/handlekurvene?** voor ar hahn`d·luh·vohng·nuh·nuh/ hahn`d·luh·kewr·vuh·nuh
Where is…?	**Hvor er…?** voor ar…

▶For food items, see page 83.

Can I have some of that/those?	**Kan jeg få litt av det/dem?** kahn yay faw liht a deh/dehm
Can I taste it?	**Kan jeg smake?** kahn yay smah`·kuh
I'd like…	**Jeg vil gjerne ha…** yay vihl yar`·nuh hah…
– a (half) kilo of…	**– en (halv) kilo…** ehn (hahl) khee´·lu…
– a (half) liter of…	**– en (halv) liter…** ehn (hahl) lee´·tuhr…
– a piece of…	**– et stykke…** eht stuik`·kuh…
– a slice of…	**– en skive…** ehn shee`·vuh…
More/Less than that.	**Mer/Mindre enn det.** mehr/mihn´·druh ehn deh
How much?	**Hvor mye koster det?** voor mew`·uh kohs`·tuhr deh
Where do I pay?	**Hvor betaler man?** voor buh·tah´·luhr mahn

| Can I have a bag? | **Kan jeg få en bærepose?** kahn yay faw ehn ba`·<u>ruh</u>·**poo**·suh |
| I'm being helped. | **Jeg blir ekspedert.** yay bleer ehks·puh·<u>**deh´**</u>rt |

▶ For conversion tables, see page 168.

You May Hear...

Kan jeg hjelpe deg? kahn yay <u>yehl´</u>·puh day	Can I help you?
Hva skal det være? vah skahl deh <u>va</u>`·ruh	What would you like?
Skal det være noe annet? skahl deh <u>va</u>`·ruh <u>noo</u>`·uh <u>ahn</u>`·nuht	Anything else?
Det blir...kroner, takk. deh bleer... <u>kroo</u>`n·uhr tahk	That's...kroner, please.

---

i In Norway, there are a few large supermarket chains, such as Rimi, Rema and Kiwi, in addition to many local "mini-markets." Keep in mind that supermarkets do not accept credit cards, so remember to bring cash when you go shopping for groceries.

Dishes, Utensils and Kitchen Tools

bottle opener	**en flaskeåpner** ehn <u>flahs</u>`·kuh·**awp**·nuhr
bowls	**skåler** <u>skaw</u>`·luhr
can opener	**en boksåpner** ehn <u>bohks</u>`·**awp**·nuhr
cheese slicer	**ostehøvel** <u>us</u>`·tuh·hur·vuhl
corkscrew	**en korketrekker** ehn <u>kohr</u>`·kuh·trehk·kuhr
cups	**kopper** <u>kohp</u>`·puhr
forks	**gafler** <u>gahf</u>´·luhr
frying pan	**en stekepanne** ehn <u>steh</u>`·kuh·pahn·nuh
glasses	**glass** glahs

knives	**kniver** <u>knee</u>v`·uhr
measuring cup/ measuring spoon	**et målebeger/en måleskje** <u>eht</u> <u>maw</u>`·luh·beh·guhr/ehn <u>maw</u>`·luh·sheh
napkins	**papirservietter** pah·<u>pee</u>´r·serv·yeht·tuhr
plates	**tallerkener** tah·<u>lehr</u>´·kuhn·uhr
pot	**en gryte** ehn <u>grui</u>`·tuh
saucepan	**en kasserolle** ehn kah·suh·<u>rohl</u>`·luh
spatula	**en slikkepott** ehn <u>slihk</u>`·kuh·poht
spoons	**skjeer** sh<u>eh</u>`·uhr

Meals

 Frokost (breakfast) is usually eaten early and consists of coffee or tea and **smørbrød** (open-faced sandwiches) and perhaps cereal. **Lunsj** (lunch) is typically a light meal and, on weekdays, may consist of a simple **matpakke** (open-faced sandwich brought from home). **Middag** (dinner) is often the only hot meal of the day. If **middag** is eaten early, then **aftens** (a late night snack), consisting of bread or crackers with butter or cheese and cold cuts, is eaten to get through the night without going hungry.

Breakfast

appelsinjuice ahp·puhl·<u>see</u>´n·yews   orange juice

appelsinmarmelade   orange marmalade
ahp·puhl·<u>see</u>´n·mahr·muh·**lah**·duh

brød brur   bread

bløtkokt/hardkokt egg <u>blur</u>`t·kukt/<u>hah</u>`r·kukt   *soft-boiled/hard-boiled*
ehg   eggs

Can I have more…?	**Kan jeg få litt mer…?** kahn yay **faw** liht m**ehr**…

egg og *bacon/skinke* ehg aw <u>*bay*</u>·kuhn/ *shihng*·kuh	eggs with *bacon/ham*
eggerøre <u>ehg</u>·guh·**rur**·ruh	scrambled eggs
frokostblanding <u>froo</u>·kohst·blahn·nihng	cereal
grapefruktjuice <u>grehp</u>·frewkt·yews	grapefruit juice
havregrøt <u>hahv</u>·ruh·grurt	oatmeal [porridge]
honning <u>hohn</u>·nihng	honey
juice yews	fruit juice
svart/koffeinfri* kaffe** *svahrt/ kohf·fuh·*ee***·n·free <u>kahf</u>·fuh	*black/decaffeinated* coffee
kaffe med *melk/fløte* <u>kahf</u>·fuh meh *mehlk/ flur*·tuh	coffee with *milk/cream*
omelett oh·muh·<u>leht</u>´	omelet
ost ust	cheese
pepper <u>pehp</u>´·puhr	pepper (seasoning)
ristet brød <u>rihs</u>·tuht brur	toast
rundstykke <u>rewn</u>´·stuik·kuh	roll
salt sahlt	salt
smør smurr	butter
speilegg <u>spayl</u>´·ehg	fried egg
syltetøy <u>suil</u>´·tuh·tury	jam
te med *melk/sitron* teh meh *mehlk/siht·<u>roo</u>´n*	tea with *milk/lemon*
varm sjokolade vahrm shu·ku·<u>lah</u>`·duh	hot chocolate
varmt vann varmt vahn	hot water
yoghurt <u>yoo</u>´·gewrt	yogurt

With/Without…	**Med/Uten…** meh/<u>ew</u>`·tuhn…
I can't have…	**Jeg tåler ikke…** yay <u>taw</u>´·luhr <u>ihk</u>`·kuh…

Appetizers [Starters]

blåskjell <u>blaw</u>`-shehl	mussels
fenalår <u>feh</u>`-nah-lawr	cured leg of mutton
ferske reker <u>fehrs</u>`-kuh <u>reh</u>`-kuhr	unshelled shrimp [prawns]
fiskekabaret <u>fihs</u>`-kuh-kah-bah-**reh**	assorted seafood and vegetables in aspic
gåselever <u>gaw</u>`-suh-leh-vuhr	goose liver
gravlaks <u>grahv</u>`-lahks	cured salmon flavored with dill
hummer <u>hum</u>´-muhr	lobster
kamskjell <u>kahm</u>`-shehl	scallop
kaviar kah-vih-**ah**´r	caviar
krabbe <u>krahb</u>`-buh	crab
laks lahks	salmon
rakørret <u>rahk</u>`-urr-ruht	specially processed, salt-cured and fermented trout
rekecocktail <u>reh</u>`-kuh-kohk-tayl	shrimp [prawn] cocktail
røkelaks <u>rur</u>`-kuh-lahks	smoked salmon
sildebrikke <u>sihl</u>`-luh-brihk-kuh	a variety of herring, served with bread and butter
skinke <u>shihng</u>`-kuh	ham
spekepølse <u>speh</u>`-kuh-purl-suh	smoked, cured sausage
spekeskinke <u>speh</u>`-kuh-shihng-kuh	smoked, cured ham
sursild <u>sewr</u>´sihl	marinated herring
østers <u>urs</u>´-tehrs	oysters

Can I have more…?	**Kan jeg få litt mer…?** kahn yay f**aw** liht m**ehr**…

Soup

aspargessuppe ahs-<u>pahr</u>´-guhs-sewp-puh	asparagus soup
betasuppe <u>beh</u>`-tah-sewp-puh	thick meat and vegetable soup
blomkålsuppe <u>blohm</u>´-kawl-sewp-puh	cauliflower soup
buljong bewl-<u>yohng</u>´	consommé
fiskesuppe <u>fihs</u>`-kuh-sewp-puh	fish soup
fransk løksuppe frahnsk <u>lur</u>`k-sewp-puh	French onion soup
grønnsaksuppe <u>grurn</u>`-s**ah**k-sewp-puh	vegetable soup
gul ertesuppe gewl <u>er</u>`-tuh-sewp-puh	yellow pea soup
hummersuppe <u>hum</u>`-muhr-sewp-puh	lobster soup
kjøttsuppe <u>khurt</u>`-sewp-puh	meat soup
løksuppe <u>lur</u>`k-sewp-puh	onion soup
neslesuppe <u>nehs</u>`-luh-sewp-puh	nettle soup
oksehalesuppe <u>ohk</u>`-suh-hah-luh-sewp-puh	oxtail soup
sellerisuppe seh-luh-<u>ree</u>´-sewp-puh	celery soup
sjampinjongsuppe shahm-pihn-<u>yohng</u>´-sewp-puh	button mushroom soup
soppsuppe <u>sohp</u>`-sewp-puh	field mushroom soup
tomatsuppe tu-<u>mah</u>´t-sewp-puh	tomato soup

Norwegian cuisine features a variety of soup, which is often eaten with **flatbrød** (a thin, barley and wheat or barley and rye cracker) as a starter to a meal. **Fiskesuppe** (fish soup) is very popular along the coast. Other traditional soups involve meat, such as **betasuppe** (meat and vegetable soup), or vegetables, like **gul ertesuppe** (yellow pea soup).

With/Without...	**Med/Uten...** meh/<u>ew</u>`-tuhn...
I can't have...	**Jeg tåler ikke...** yay <u>taw</u>´-luhr <u>ihk</u>`-kuh...

Fish and Seafood

abbor <u>ahb`</u>·bohr	perch
akkar <u>ahk`</u>·kahr	squid
ansjos ahn·<u>shoo</u>´s	anchovies or marinated sprats
blåskjell <u>blaw`</u>·shehl	mussels
blekksprut <u>blehk`</u>·sprewt	octopus
brasme <u>brahs`</u>·muh	bream
breiflabb <u>bray`</u>·flahb	angler, also called frogfish or goosefish
dampet ørret <u>dahm`</u>·puht <u>urr`</u>·ruht	poached trout
fisk fihsk	fish
fiskeboller <u>fihs`</u>·kuh·bohl·luhr	fish balls
fiskekaker <u>fihs`</u>·kuh·**kah**·kuhr	fried fish cakes
fiskepudding <u>fihs`</u>·kuh·pewd·dihng	fish pudding
flyndre <u>fluin`</u>·druh	flounder
fritert flyndrefilet friht·<u>**eh**´r</u>t <u>fluin`</u>·druh·fih·**leh**	deep fried flounder fillet
gjedde <u>yehd`</u>·duh	pike
gravlaks <u>grah`</u>v·lahks	cured salmon flavored with dill
hellefisk <u>hehl`</u>·luh·fihsk	halibut
hummer <u>hum´</u>·muhr	lobster
hvitting <u>viht`</u>·tihng	whiting
hyse <u>hui`</u>·suh	haddock (western Norway)
kamskjell <u>kahm`</u>·shel	scallop

Can I have more…?	**Kan jeg få litt mer…?** kahn yay f**aw** liht m**ehr**…

karpe <u>kahr</u>`·puh	carp
klippfisk <u>klihp</u>´·fihsk	salted and dried fish
kokt torsk kukt tohrsk	poached cod
kokt ørret kukt <u>urr</u>`·ruht	poached trout
kolje <u>kohl</u>`·yuh	haddock (eastern Norway)
krabbe <u>krahb</u>`·buh	crab
kreps krehps	freshwater crayfish
kveite <u>kvay</u>`·tuh	halibut
laks lahks	salmon
lutefisk <u>lew</u>`·tuh·fihsk	stockfish soaked in lye
lysing <u>luï</u>`·sihng	hake
makrell mahk·<u>rehl</u>´	mackerel
piggvar <u>pihg</u>`·vahr	turbot
plukkfisk <u>pluk</u>´·fihsk	stewed codfish
regnbueørret <u>rayn</u>`·b**ew**·uh·urr·ruht	rainbow trout
reker <u>reh</u>`·kuhr	shrimp [prawns]
rogn rohngn	roe
rødspette <u>rur</u>`·speht·tuh	plaice
sardell sar·<u>dehl</u>´	canned anchovy
sardin sar·<u>dee</u>´n	sardine
sei say	pollock
sik s**ee**k	whitefish
sild sihl	herring
sjømat <u>shur</u>`·m**ah**t	seafood

With/Without…	**Med/Uten…** meh/<u>ew</u>`·tuhn…
I can't have…	**Jeg tåler ikke…** yay <u>taw</u>´·luhr <u>ihk</u>`·kuh…

sjøørret <u>shur</u>`·urr·ruht	sea trout
sjøtunge <u>shur</u>`·tung·uh	sole
skalldyr <u>skahl</u>`·duir	shellfish
spekesild <u>speh</u>`·kuh·sihl	salted herring
steinbit <u>stayn</u>`·beet	catfish
stør sturr	sturgeon
størje <u>sturr</u>`·yuh	tuna
torsk tohrsk	cod
tunfisk <u>tew</u>`n·fihsk	tuna
tørrfisk <u>turr</u>`·fihsk	stockfish
uer <u>ew</u>`·uhr	rosefish
ørret <u>urr</u>`·ruht	trout
østers <u>urs</u>`·tehrs	oysters
åbor <u>aw</u>`·bohr	perch
ål awl	eel

Can I have more…? **Kan jeg få litt mer…?** kahn yay f<u>aw</u> liht mehr…

Meat and Poultry

and ahn — duck

bacon bay´-kuhn — bacon

benløse fugler beh`n-lurs-uh few´l-uhr — fried, rolled and stuffed slices of veal or beef

biff bihf — beef steak

biff med løk bihf meh lurk — thick beef steak topped with fried onion

broiler broi´-luhr — chicken

brun lapskaus brewn lahps´-kevs — Norwegian stew in brown gravy

dyrestek dui`-ruh-stehk — roast venison

elg ehlg — moose

elgbiff ehlg`-bihf — moose steak

elgfilet ehlg`-fih-leh — moose fillet

elgstek ehlg`-stehk — roast moose

fårestek faw`-ruh-stehk — roast leg of mutton or lamb

fårekjøtt faw`-ruh-khurt — mutton

fårikål faw´-rih-kawl — mutton or lamb in cabbage stew

fasan fah-sah´n — pheasant

gås gaws — goose

hare hah`-ruh — hare

With/Without... **Med/Uten...** meh/ew´-tuhn...

I can't have... **Jeg tåler ikke...** yay taw´-luhr ihk`-kuh...

hjort yohrt	deer
høne <u>hur</u>`·nuh	hen
hvalbiff <u>vahl</u>`·bihf	whale steak
kalkun kahl·<u>kew</u>´n	turkey
kalvebrissel <u>kahl</u>`·vuh·brihs·suhl	calf's sweetbread
kalvekjøtt <u>kahl</u>`·vuh·khurt	veal
kalvelever <u>kahl</u>`·vuh·lehv·vuhr	calf's liver
kanin kah·<u>nee</u>´n	rabbit
karbonade kahr·bu·<u>nah</u>`·duh	hamburger
kjøttboller khurt	meatballs
kjøttkaker <u>khurt</u>`·**kahk**·uhr	small hamburgers
kjøttpudding <u>khurt</u>`·pud·dihng	meatloaf
knoke <u>knoo</u>`·kuh	bone
kotelett koh·tuh·<u>leht</u>´	chop
kylling <u>khuil</u>`·lihng	chicken
lammekjøtt <u>lahm</u>`·muh·khurt	lamb
lapskaus <u>lahps</u>´·kehvs	Norwegian stew with meat, potatoes and root vegetables
lever <u>lehv</u>´·vuhr	liver
lys lapskaus luis <u>lahps</u>´·kehvs	Norwegian stew with diced, salted boiled pork
medisterkaker meh·<u>dihs</u>´·tuhr·**kah**·kuhr	small pork and beef hamburgers
medisterpølse meh·<u>dihs</u>´·tuhr·purl·suh	pork and beef sausage

Can I have more…?	**Kan jeg få litt mer…?** kahn yay f**aw** liht m**ehr**…

70

mørbradstek <u>mur`</u>r·brahd·stehk	roast sirloin
nyrer <u>nui`</u>·ruhr	kidneys
oksebryst <u>ohk`</u>·suh·bruist	beef brisket
oksekjøtt <u>ohk`</u>·suh·khurt	beef
okserulader <u>ohk`</u>·suh·rewl·**lah**·duhr	braised beef rolls
oksestek <u>ohk`</u>·suh·stehk	roast beef
orrfugl <u>ohr`</u>·fewl	black grouse, a woodland bird
pinnekjøtt <u>pihn`</u>·nuh·khurt	salted and dried mutton ribs steamed on twigs
pytt i panne puit·ih·<u>pah`</u>·nuh	hash or meat and vegetables
pølse <u>purl`</u>·suh	sausage
rådyr <u>raw´</u>·duir	roe-deer
rapphøne <u>rahp`</u>·hur·nuh	partridge
reinsdyr <u>rayns´</u>·duir	reindeer
ribbe <u>rihb`</u>·buh	spareribs
rype <u>rui`</u>·puh	grouse, a mountain bird
skinke <u>shihng`</u>·kuh	ham
spekeskinke <u>speh`</u>·kuh·shihng·kuh	smoked, cured ham
-stek stehk	roast (beef, reindeer, moose, etc.)
svinekjøtt <u>svee´</u>·nuh·khurt	pork
svor svoor	bacon rind [crackling]

With/Without…	**Med/Uten…** meh/<u>**ew`**</u>·tuhn…
I can't have…	**Jeg tåler ikke…** yay <u>taw´</u>·luhr <u>ihk`</u>·kuh…

sylte <u>suil'</u>·tuh	head cheese [brawn]
tartarbiff tahr·<u>tah'r</u>·bihf	steak tartare
T-benstek <u>teh'</u>·behn·stehk	T-bone steak
vaktel <u>vahk'</u>·tuhl	quail
villand <u>vihl'</u>·lahn	wild duck
wienerschnitzel <u>vee'</u>·nuhr·shniht·suhl	breaded veal cutlet

rare	**råstekt** <u>raw'</u>·stehkt	
medium	**medium stekt** <u>meh'</u>·dih·ewm stehkt	
well-done	**godt stekt** goht stehkt	

Vegetables and Staples

agurk ah·<u>gewr'k</u>	cucumber
artisjokker ar·tih·<u>shohk'</u>·kuhr	artichokes
asparges ahs·<u>pahr'</u>·guhs	asparagus
aubergine aw·buhr·<u>shee'n</u>	eggplant [aubergine]
blomkål <u>blohm'</u>·kawl	cauliflower
bønner <u>burn`</u>·nuhr	beans
brokkoli <u>brohk'</u>·koh·lih	broccoli
erter <u>ehr'</u>·tuhr	peas
gresskar <u>grehs`</u>·kahr	pumpkin
grønnkål <u>grurn'</u>·kawl	kale
gulrøtter <u>gew`l</u>·rurt·tuhr	carrots
hodesalat <u>hoo`</u>·duh·sah·laht	lettuce

Can I have more…?	**Kan jeg få litt mer…?** kahn yay f**aw** liht m**eh**r…

kål kawl	cabbage
kantareller kahn·tah·<u>rehl</u>´·luhr	chanterelle mushrooms
kokte poteter <u>kuk</u>`·tuh pu·<u>teh</u>´t·uhr	boiled potatoes
komler/komper <u>kum</u>`·luhr/<u>kum</u>`·puhr	potato dumplings
linser <u>lihn</u>`·suhr	lentils
løk lurk	onions
mais mies	corn
maiskolbe mies´·kohl·buh	corn on the cob
nepe <u>neh</u>`·puh	turnip
nudler <u>newd</u>´·luhr	noodles
nypoteter <u>nui</u>`·pu·<u>teht</u>·uhr	new potatoes
paprika <u>pahp</u>´·rih·kah	sweet pepper
pommes frites pohm friht	French fries [chips]
potet pu·<u>teh</u>´t	potato
potetgull pu·<u>teh</u>´t·gewl	potato chips [crisps]
potetkroketter pu·<u>teh</u>´t·krohk·keht·tuhr	potato croquettes
potetmos pu·<u>teh</u>´t·moos	mashed potatoes
potetsalat pu·<u>teh</u>´t·sah·<u>laht</u>	potato salad
purre <u>pewr</u>`·ruh	leeks
raspeball <u>rahs</u>`·puh·bahl	potato dumplings
reddiker <u>rehd</u>´·dihk·kuhr	radishes
ris rees	rice
rosenkål <u>roo</u>´·suhn·kawl	Brussels sprouts

With/Without…	**Med/Uten…** meh/<u>**ew**</u>`·tuhn…
I can't have…	**Jeg tåler ikke…** yay <u>taw</u>´·luhr <u>ihk</u>`·kuh…

rødbeter <u>rur</u>`·beh·tuhr	beet [beetroot]
rødkål <u>rur</u>´·kawl	red cabbage
salat sah·<u>lah</u>´t	salad
selleri sehl·luhr·<u>ee</u>´	celery
sildeball <u>sihl</u>`·luh·bahl	potato dumplings filled with minced salted herring
stekte poteter <u>stehk</u>`·tuh pu·<u>teh</u>´t·uhr	sautéed potatoes
stuede poteter <u>stew</u>`·eh·duh pu·<u>teh</u>´t·uhr	potatoes in a white sauce
sjampinjonger sham·pihn·<u>yohng</u>´·uhr	button mushrooms
sopp sohp	mushrooms
spinat spih·<u>nah</u>´t	spinach
surkål <u>sew</u>´r·kawl	coleslaw
sylteagurk <u>suil</u>`·tuh·ah·gewrk	pickle
tomater tu·<u>maht</u>´·uhr	tomatoes

Spices

anisfrø <u>ah</u>´·nihs·frur	aniseed
basilikum bah·<u>see</u>´·lih·kewm	basil
dill dihl	dill
einebær <u>ay</u>`·nuh·bar	juniper berries
gressløk <u>grehs</u>`·lurk	chives
hvitløk <u>vee</u>´t·lurk	garlic
ingefær <u>ihng</u>´·uh·far	ginger
kanel kah·<u>neh</u>´l	cinnamon

Can I have more…?	**Kan jeg få litt mer…?** kahn yay **faw** liht **mehr**…

kapers <u>kah</u>´·puhrs	capers
karri <u>kahr</u>´·rih	curry seasoning
karve <u>kahr</u>`·vuh	caraway seeds
nellik <u>nehl</u>´·lihk	clove
pepper <u>pehp</u>´·puhr	pepper (seasoning)
persille pehr·<u>sihl</u>´·luh	parsley
salt sahlt	salt
salvie sahl·<u>vee</u>`·uh	sage
timian <u>tee</u>´·mih·ahn	thyme

Fruit and Nuts

ananas <u>ahn</u>´·nah·nahs	pineapple
appelsin ahp·puhl·<u>see</u>´n	orange
aprikos ahp·rih·<u>koo</u>´s	apricot
banan bah·<u>nah</u>´n	banana
bjørnebær <u>byur</u>`·nuh·bar	blackberries
blåbær <u>blaw</u>`·bar	blueberries
bringebær <u>brihng</u>´·uh·bar	raspberries
dadler <u>dahd</u>´·luhr	dates
druer <u>drew</u>`·uhr	grapes
eple <u>ehp</u>`·luh	apple
fersken <u>fehrs</u>´·kuhn	peach
fikener <u>fee</u>´·kuhn·uhr	figs
grapefrukt <u>grehp</u>´·frewkt	grapefruit
hasselnøtter <u>hahs</u>´·suhl·nurt·tuhr	hazelnuts

With/Without…	**Med/Uten…** meh/<u>ew</u>`·tuhn…
I can't have…	**Jeg tåler ikke…** yay <u>taw</u>´·luhr <u>ihk</u>`·kuh…

jordbær <u>yoo´r</u>·bar	strawberries
kastanjer kahs·<u>tahn´</u>·yuhr	chestnuts
kirsebær <u>khihr´</u>·suh·bar	cherries
kokosnøtt <u>kuk´</u>·kus·nurt	coconut
korinter ku·<u>rihn´</u>·tuhr	currants
mandarin mahn·dah·<u>ree´n</u>	tangerine
mandler <u>mahn´d</u>·luhr	almonds
markjordbær <u>mahr´k</u>·<u>yoor</u>·bar	wild strawberries
melon meh·<u>loo´n</u>	melon
molter/multer <u>mohl`</u>·tuhr/mewl`·tuhr	arctic cloudberries
moreller mu·<u>rehl´</u>·luhr	morello cherries
nektarin nehk·tah·<u>ree´n</u>	nectarine
nøtter <u>nurt´</u>·tuhr	nuts
peanøtter <u>pee´</u>·ah·nurt·tuhr	peanuts
plommer <u>plum`</u>·muhr	plums
pære <u>pa`</u>·ruh	pear
rabarbra rah·<u>bahr´</u>·brah	rhubarb
rips rihps	red currants
rognebær <u>rohng`</u>·nuh·bar	rowanberries
rosiner ru·<u>see´</u>·nuhr	raisins
sitron siht·<u>roo´n</u>	lemon
solbær <u>soo`l</u>·bar	black currants
stikkelsbær <u>stihk´</u>·kuhls·bar	gooseberries
svisker <u>svihs`</u>·kuhr	prunes
tranebær <u>trah`</u>·nuh·bar	cranberries

Can I have more…?	**Kan jeg få litt mer…?** kahn yay f**aw** liht m**ehr**…

tyttebær <u>tuit'</u>·tuh·bar	lingonberry
valnøtter <u>vahl'</u>·nurt·tuhr	walnuts
vannmelon <u>vahn'</u>·meh·<u>loo</u>n	watermelon

Cheese

ekte geitost <u>ehk'</u>·tuh <u>yayt'</u>·ust	goat cheese
fløtemysost <u>flur'</u>·tuh·muis·ust	mild and sweet cow's milk cheese
gammelost <u>gahm'</u>·muhl·ust	pungent cheese made with skimmed milk
gudbrandsdalsost <u>gewd'</u>·brahns·dahls·ust	cow and goat's milk cheese
jarlsbergost <u>yahrls'</u>·behrg·ust	mild, slightly sweet, semi-hard cheese
normannaost noor·<u>mahn'</u>·nah·ust	blue-veined cow's milk cheese
ridderost <u>rihd'</u>·duhr·ust	semi-hard cheese with nutty flavor

Dessert

bløtkake <u>blur't</u>·kah·kuh	layer cake
fruktkompott <u>frewkt'</u>·kohm·poht	stewed fruit
hoffdessert <u>hohf'</u>·dehs·sar	layers of meringue and whipped cream, topped with chocolate sauce and toasted almonds
is ees	ice cream

With/Without…	**Med/Uten…** meh/<u>ew'</u>·tuhn…
I can't have…	**Jeg tåler ikke…** yay <u>taw'</u>·luhr <u>ihk'</u>·kuh…

karamellpudding kah·rah·**mehl**´·pewd·dihng	creme caramel
krem kr**eh**m	whipped cream
mandelkake <u>mahn</u>´·duhl·**kah**·kuh	almond cake
molter/multer med krem <u>mohl</u>`·tuhr/ mewl`tuhr meh kr**eh**m	arctic cloudberries with whipped cream
pære Belle Helene <u>pa</u>`·ruh behl heh·**leh**´n	poached pears with vanilla ice cream and chocolate
pannekaker <u>pahn</u>`·nuh·**kah**·kuhr	pancakes
riskrem <u>ree</u>´s·kr**eh**m	creamed rice
rødgrøt med fløte <u>rur</u>`·grurt meh <u>flur</u>`·tuh	berry compote with cream
sjokoladepudding shu·ku·<u>lah</u>`·duh·pewd·dihng	chocolate pudding
sorbett sohr·<u>beht</u>´	sorbet
sufflé sewf·<u>leh</u>´	soufflé
terte <u>tehr</u>`·tuh	fruit cake
tilslørte bondepiker <u>tihl</u>´·sl**u**rr·tuh <u>bun</u>´·nuh·**pee**·kuhr	layers of stewed apples, cookie [biscuit] crumbs, and whipped cream
vafler med syltetøy <u>vahf</u>´·luhr meh <u>suil</u>`·tuh·tury	waffles with jam
vaniljesaus vah·<u>nihl</u>`·yuh·sevs	vanilla sauce
varm eplekake med krem vahrm <u>ehp</u>`·luh·**kah**·kuh meh kr**eh**m	hot apple pie with whipped cream

Can I have more...?	**Kan jeg få litt mer...?** kahn yay f**aw** liht m**eh**r...
With/Without...	**Med/Uten...** meh/<u>ew</u>`·tuhn...
I can't have...	**Jeg tåler ikke...** yay <u>taw</u>´·luhr <u>ihk</u>`·kuh...

78

Essential

Can I have the *wine list/drink menu*?	**Kan jeg få se *vinkartet/drikkekartet*?** kahn yay faw seh <u>veen</u>`·kahr·tuh/<u>drihk</u>`·kuh·kahr·tuh
What do you recommend?	**Hva kan du anbefale?** vah kahn dew <u>ahn</u>´·buh·fah·luh
Can I have the house wine?	**Kan jeg få husets vin?** kahn yay faw <u>hew's</u>·uhs veen
Can I buy you a drink?	**Kan jeg by på en drink?** kahn yay bui poh ehn drihngk
Cheers!	**Skål!** skawl
A *coffee/tea*, please.	**En *kaffe/te*, takk.** ehn <u>kahf</u>´·fuh/**teh** tahk
Black.	**Svart.** svahrt
With...	**Med...** meh...
– milk	**– melk** mehlk
– sugar	**– sukker** <u>suk</u>´·kuhr
– artificial sweetener	**– søtningsmiddel** <u>sur</u>`t·nihngs·mihd·duhl
A glass of..., please.	**Et glass..., takk.** eht glahs...tahk
– juice	**– juice** yews
– soda	**– soda** <u>soo</u>´·dah
– (*sparkling/still*) water	**– vann (*med kullsyre/uten kullsyre*)** vahn (meh <u>kewl</u>´·sui·ruh/<u>**ew**</u>´·tuhn <u>kewl</u>´·sui·ruh)
Is the tap water safe to drink?	**Kan man drikke vann rett fra springen?** kahn mahn <u>drihk</u>`·kuh vahn reht frah <u>sprihng</u>´·uhn

Non-alcoholic Drinks

ananasjuice ahn´·nah·nahs·yews	pineapple juice
appelsinjuice ahp·puhl·see´n·yews	orange juice
brus brews	soda
eplesaft eh`·pluh·sahft	apple juice
grapefruktjuice grehp´·frewkt·yews	grapefruit juice
iste ee`s·teh	iced tea
lettmelk leht´·mehlk	low-fat milk
melk mehlk	milk
mineralvann *med kullsyre/uten kullsyre* mih·nuh·rahl´·vahn meh kewl`·sui·ruh/ew`·tuhn kewl`·sui·ruh	*sparkling/still* mineral water
sitronbrus siht·roo´n·brews	lemonade

 If you're not in the mood for Norwegian beer or spirits, there are a number of other drinks to enjoy. Tea and especially strong coffee are commonly drunk throughout the day. For soft drinks you could try **Solo** (orange-flavored soda) or **Mozell** (apple-flavored soda).

You May Hear...

Hva vil du ha å drikke? vah vihl dew hah aw drihk`·kuh	What would you like to drink?
Med eller uten kullsyre? meh ehl´·luhr ew`·tuhn kewl`·sui·ruh	Sparkling or still water?

Aperitifs, Cocktails and Liqueurs

akevitt ah·kuh·<u>viht</u>′	aquavit
brandy <u>brehn</u>′·dih	brandy
gin tonic dshihn <u>tohn</u>′·nihk	gin and tonic
konjakk kohn·<u>yahk</u>′	cognac
likør lih·<u>kur</u>′r	liqueur
portvin <u>poort</u>′·veen	port
rom rum	rum
sherry <u>sher</u>′·rih	sherry
vermut <u>vehr</u>′·mewt	vermouth
vodka <u>vohd</u>′·kah	vodka
whisky <u>vihs</u>′·kih	whisky

Beer

fatøl <u>fah</u>`t·url	draft [draught] beer
flaskeøl <u>flahs</u>`·kuh·url	bottled beer
lyst/mørkt **øl** *l<u>ui</u>st/murrkt* url	*light/dark* beer
pils pihls	lager
utenlandsk øl <u>ew</u>`·tuhn·lahnsk url	imported beer

Beer in Norway is classified by strength. **Lettøl** (beer with low alcohol content) is less than 2.5% alcohol content and **zero** and **vørterøl** are both non-alcoholic. **Pils** (lager) and **bayerøl** (medium-strength dark beer) are relatively low in alcohol content. The strongest beers (6–10%), like **eksportøl** (strong light beer) and **bokkøl** (strong dark beer), are only sold at the **Vinmonopolet** (state-run liquor store).

If you are in Norway around Christmas time, be sure to try some of the special limited-edition Christmas brews which are extremely popular with the locals.

Beer, in addition to being drunk on its own, often serves as a chaser to **akevitt** (aquavit), an extremely potent drink distilled from potato and caraway seeds.

Wine

avkjølt <u>ah</u>´v·khurlt	chilled
champagne shahm·<u>pahn</u>´·yuh	champagne
fyldig <u>fuil</u>`·dih	full-bodied
hvitvin <u>veet</u>´·veen	white
meget tørr <u>meh</u>`·guht turr	very dry
musserende mews·<u>seh</u>´·ruh·nuh	sparkling
rødvin <u>rur</u>´·veen	red
rosévin roo·<u>seh</u>´·veen	rosé
søt surt	sweet

Menu Reader

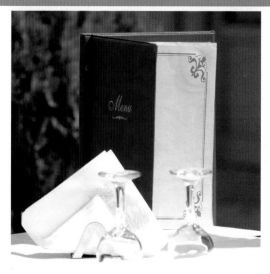

abbor <u>ahb</u>`·bohr	perch
agurk ah·<u>gewr´</u>k	cucumber
akevitt ah·kuh·<u>viht´</u>	aquavit
akkar <u>ahk</u>`·kahr	squid
and ahn	duck
ananas <u>ahn´</u>·nah·nahs	pineapple
ananasjuice <u>ahn´</u>·nah·nahs·<u>yew</u>s	pineapple juice
anisfrø <u>ah´</u>·nihs·frur	aniseed
ansjos ahn·<u>shoo´</u>s	anchovies or marinated sprats
appelsin ahp·puhl·<u>see´</u>n	orange

appelsinjuice ahp·puhl·<u>see´n</u>·yews — orange juice

appelsinmarmelade ahp·puhl·<u>see´n</u>·mahr·muh·<u>**lah**</u>·duh — orange marmalade

aprikos ahp·rih·<u>koo´s</u> — apricot

artisjokker ar·tih·<u>shohk´</u>·kuhr — artichokes

asparges ahs·<u>pahr´</u>·guhs — asparagus

aspargessuppe ahs·<u>pahr´</u>·guhs·sewp·puh — asparagus soup

aubergine aw·buhr·<u>shee´n</u> — eggplant [aubergine]

bacon <u>bay´</u>·kuhn — bacon

banan bah·<u>nah´n</u> — banana

basilikum bah·<u>see´</u>·lih·kewm — basil

benløse fugler <u>beh´n</u>·lurs·uh <u>few´l</u>·uhr — fried, rolled and stuffed slices of veal or beef

betasuppe <u>beh`</u>·tah·sewp·puh — thick meat and vegetable soup

biff bihf — beef steak

bjørnebær <u>byur´r</u>·nuh·bar — blackberries

blomkål <u>blohm´</u>·kawl — cauliflower

blomkålsuppe <u>blohm´</u>·kawl·sewp·puh — cauliflower soup

bløtkake <u>blur`t</u>·kah·kuh — layer cake

blåbær <u>blaw`</u>·bar — blueberries

blåskjell <u>blaw`</u>·shehl — mussels

blekksprut <u>blehk´</u>·sprewt — octopus

brandy <u>brehn´</u>·dih — brandy

brasme <u>brahs`</u>·muh — bream

brekkbønner <u>brehk´</u>·burn·nuhr — French beans

bringebær <u>brihng´</u>·uh·bar — raspberries

broiler <u>broi´</u>·luhr — chicken

brokkoli <u>brohk</u>´·koh·lih	broccoli
brisling <u>brihs</u>`·lihng	sprat, brisling
brun lapskaus brewn <u>lahps</u>´·kevs	Norwegian stew in brown gravy
brus brews	soda
brød br<u>ur</u>	bread
buljong bewl·<u>yohng</u>´	consommé
bønner <u>burn</u>`·nuhr	beans
dadler <u>dahd</u>´·luhr	dates
dill dihl	dill
druer <u>drew</u>`·uhr	grapes
dyrestek <u>dui</u>´·ruh·st<u>eh</u>k	roast venison
egg <u>eh</u>g	eggs
eggerøre <u>ehg</u>`·guh·<u>rur</u>·ruh	scrambled eggs
einebær <u>ay</u>`·nuh·bar	juniper berries
ekte geitost <u>ehk</u>`·tuh <u>yayt</u>`·ust	goat cheese
elg <u>eh</u>lg	moose
elgbiff <u>ehlg</u>`·bihf	moose steak
elgfilet <u>ehlg</u>`·fih·l<u>eh</u>	fillet of moose
elgstek <u>ehlg</u>`·st<u>eh</u>k	roast moose
eple <u>ehp</u>`·luh	apple
eplekake <u>ehp</u>`·luh·<u>kah</u>·kuh	apple pie
eplesaft <u>eh</u>`·pluh·sahft	apple juice
erter <u>ehr</u>´·tuhr	peas
fasan fah·<u>sah</u>´n	pheasant
fatøl <u>fah</u>`t·url	draft [draught] beer
fenalår <u>feh</u>`·nah·lawr	cured leg of mutton
fersken <u>fehrs</u>´·kuhn	peach

fikener <u>fee</u>`·kuhn·uhr	figs
fisk fihsk	fish
fiskeboller <u>fihs</u>`·kuh·bohl·luhr	fish balls
fiskekabaret <u>fihs</u>`·kuh·kah·bah·reh	assorted seafood and vegetables in aspic
fiskepudding <u>fihs</u>`·kuh·pewd·dihng	fish pudding
fiskesuppe <u>fihs</u>`·kuh·sewp·puh	fish soup
flyndre <u>fluin</u>`·druh	flounder
fløtemysost <u>flur</u>`·tuh·<u>muis</u>·ust	mild and sweet cow's milk cheese
fransk løksuppe frahnsk <u>lur</u>`k·sewp·puh	French onion soup
frokostblanding froo´·kohst·blahn·nihng	cereal
fruktkompott frewkt´·kohm·poht	stewed fruit
fårekjøtt <u>faw</u>`·ruh·khurt	mutton
fårestek <u>faw</u>`·ruh·stehk	roast leg of mutton or lamb
fårikål <u>faw</u>´·rih·kawl	mutton or lamb in cabbage stew
gammelost <u>gahm</u>`·muhl·ust	pungent cheese made with skimmed milk
gin tonic dshihn <u>tohn</u>´·nihk	gin and tonic
gjedde <u>yehd</u>`·duh	pike
grapefrukt <u>grehp</u>´·frewkt	grapefruit
grapefruktjuice <u>grehp</u>´·frewkt·y**ews**	grapefruit juice
gravlaks <u>grah</u>`v·lahks	cured salmon flavored with dill
gresskar <u>grehs</u>`·k**ahr**	pumpkin
gressløk <u>grehs</u>`·l**ur**k	chives
grønnkål <u>grurn</u>´·k**awl**	kale

grønnsaksuppe <u>grurn</u>`·sahk·sewp·puh	vegetable soup
gudbrandsdalsost <u>gewd</u>`·brahns·dahls·ust	cow and goat's milk cheese
gul ertesuppe gewl <u>er</u>`·tuh·sewp·puh	yellow pea soup
gulrøtter <u>gew</u>`l·rurt·tuhr	carrots
gås gaws	goose
gåselever <u>gaw</u>`·suh·leh·vuhr	goose liver
hare <u>hah</u>`·ruh	hare
harestek <u>hah</u>`·ruh·stehk	roast hare
hasselnøtter <u>hahs</u>´·suhl·nurt·tuhr	hazelnuts
havregrøt <u>hahv</u>`·ruh·grurt	porridge
hellefisk <u>hehl</u>`·luh·fihsk	halibut
hjort yohrt	deer
hjortesadel <u>yohr</u>`·tuh·<u>sah</u>·duhl	saddle of deer
hodesalat <u>hoo</u>`·duh·sah·<u>laht</u>	lettuce
hoffdessert <u>hohf</u>´·dehs·sar	layers of meringue and whipped cream, topped with chocolate sauce and toasted almonds
honning <u>hohn</u>`·nihng	honey
hummer <u>hum</u>´·muhr	lobster
hvalbiff <u>vahl</u>`·bihf	whale steak
hvitløk <u>vee</u>´t·lurk	garlic
hvitting <u>viht</u>`·tihng	whiting
hvitvin <u>veet</u>´·veen	white wine
hyse <u>hui</u>`·suh	haddock (western Norway)
høne <u>hur</u>`·nuh	hen

ingefær <u>ihng</u>´·uh·far	ginger
is <u>ee</u>s	ice cream
iste <u>ee</u>`s·teh	iced tea
jarlsbergost <u>yahrls</u>´·behrg·ust	mild, slightly sweet, semi-hard cheese
jordbær <u>yoor</u>´·bar	strawberries
juice <u>yew</u>s	fruit juice
kaffe <u>kahf</u>´·fuh	coffee
kalkun kahl·<u>kew</u>´n	turkey
kalvebrissel <u>kahl</u>`·vuh·brihs·suhl	calf's sweetbread
kalvekjøtt <u>kahl</u>`·vuh·khurt	veal
kalvemedaljonger <u>kahl</u>`·vuh·meh·dahl·yohng·uhr	small round fillet of veal
kalvelever <u>kahl</u>`·vuh·lehv·vuhr	calf's liver
kamskjell <u>kahm</u>`·shel	scallop
kanel kah·<u>neh</u>´l	cinnamon
kanin kah·<u>nee</u>´n	rabbit
kapers <u>kah</u>´·puhrs	capers
karbonade kahr·bu·<u>nah</u>`·duh	hamburger
karpe <u>kahr</u>`·puh	carp
kastanjer kahs·<u>tahn</u>´·yuhr	chestnuts
karri <u>kahr</u>´·rih	curry seasoning
karve <u>kahr</u>`·vuh	caraway seeds
kaviar kah·vih·<u>ah</u>´r	caviar
kirsebær <u>khihr</u>´·suh·bar	cherries
kjøttboller <u>khurt</u>`·bohl·uhr	meatballs
kjøttkaker <u>khurt</u>`·<u>kahk</u>·uhr	small hamburgers
kjøttpudding <u>khurt</u>`·pud·dihng	meatloaf

kjøttsuppe <u>khurt</u>`·sewp·puh	meat soup
klippfisk <u>klihp</u>´·fihsk	salted and dried cod
knoke <u>kn**oo**</u>`·kuh	bone
kokosnøtt <u>kuk</u>´·kus·nurt	coconut
kolje <u>kohl</u>`·yuh	haddock (eastern Norway)
korinter ku·<u>rihn</u>´·tuhr	currants
kotelett koh·tuh·<u>leht</u>´	chop
krabbe <u>krahb</u>`·buh	crab
kreps krehps	freshwater crayfish
kveite <u>kvay</u>`·tuh	halibut
kylling <u>khuil</u>`·lihng	chicken
kål kawl	cabbage
kålrabi/kålrot kawl·<u>rah</u>´·bih/<u>kawl</u>`·root	rutabaga [swede BE]
kantareller kahn·tah·<u>rehl</u>´·luhr	chanterelle mushrooms
karamellpudding kah·rah·<u>mehl</u>´·pewd·dihng	creme caramel
kokte poteter <u>kuk</u>`·tuh pu·<u>teh</u>´t·uhr	boiled potatoes
komler/komper <u>kum</u>`·luhr/<u>kum</u>`·puhr	potato dumplings (western Norway)
konjakk kohn·<u>yahk</u>´	cognac
krem kr**eh**m	whipped cream
laks lahks	salmon
lammebog <u>lahm</u>`·muh·b**oo**g	shoulder of lamb
lammebryst <u>lahm</u>`·muh·bruist	brisket of lamb
lammekjøtt <u>lahm</u>`·muh·khurt	lamb
lammelår <u>lahm</u>`·muh·**lawr**	leg of lamb
lammesadel <u>lahm</u>`·muh·s**ah**·duhl	saddle of lamb

lammestek <u>lahm</u>`·muh·st**eh**k	roast lamb
lapskaus <u>lahps</u>´·kevs	Norwegian stew with meat, potatoes and vegetables
lettmelk <u>leht</u>`·mehlk	low-fat milk
lever <u>lehv</u>´·vuhr	liver
likør lih·<u>kur</u>´r	liqueur
linser <u>lihn</u>`·suhr	lentils
lungemos <u>lung</u>`·uh·m**oos**	ground [minced] lungs and onions
lutefisk <u>lew</u>`·tuh·fihsk	stockfish soaked in lye
lys lapskaus l**u**is <u>lahps</u>´·kevs	Norwegian stew with diced, salted and boiled pork
løk l**u**rk	onions
løksuppe <u>lur</u>`k·sewp·puh	onion soup
mais m**ie**s	corn
maiskolbe <u>mies</u>´·kohl·buh	corn on the cob
mandarin mahn·dah·<u>ree</u>´n	tangerine
mandelkake <u>mahn</u>´·duhl·**kah**·kuh	almond cake
mandler <u>mahn´d</u>·luhr	almonds
makrell mahk·<u>rehl</u>´	mackerel
markjordbær <u>mahr</u>`k·y**oo**r·bar	wild strawberries
medisterkaker meh·<u>dihs</u>´·tuhr·**kah**·kuhr	small pork and beef hamburgers
medisterpølse meh·<u>dihs</u>´·tuhr·purl·suh	pork and beef sausage
melk mehlk	milk
melon meh·<u>loo</u>´n	melon

milkshake mihlk´·shayk — milkshake

mineralvann mih·nuh·**rahl**´·vahn — mineral water

molter/multer mohl´·tuhr/mewl´·tuhr — arctic cloudberries

moreller mu·**rehl**´·luhr — morello cherries

mørbradstek mur´r·brahd·stehk — roast sirloin

nektarin nehk·tah·**ree**´n — nectarine

nellik nehl´·lihk — clove

neslesuppe nehs`·luh·sewp·puh — nettle soup

nepe neh`·puh — turnip

normannaost noor·**mahn**´·nah·ust — blue-veined cow's milk cheese

nudler newd´·luhr — noodles

nypoteter nui`·pu·**teht**·uhr — new potatoes

nyrer nui`·ruhr — kidneys

nøtter nurt´·tuhr — nuts

oksebryst ohk`·suh·bruist — brisket of beef

oksefilet ohk`·suh·fih·**leh** — fillet of beef

oksehalesuppe ohk`·suh·hah·luh·sewp·puh — oxtail soup

oksekam ohk`·suh·kahm — loin

oksekjøtt ohk`·suh·khurt — beef

okserulader ohk`·suh·rewl·l**ah**·duhr — braised beef rolls

oksestek ohk`·suh·stehk — roast beef

omelett oh·muh·**leht**´ — omelet

orrfugl ohr`·fewl — black grouse, a woodland bird

ost ust — cheese

pannekaker pahn`·nuh·k**ah**·kuhr — pancakes

paprika pahp´·rih·kah — sweet pepper

peanøtter <u>pee</u>´·ah·nurt·tuhr	peanuts
pepper <u>pehp</u>´·puhr	pepper
persille pehr·<u>sihl</u>´·luh	parsley
piggvar <u>pihg</u>`·vahr	turbot
pils pihls	lager
pinnekjøtt <u>pihn</u>`·nuh·khurt	salted and dried mutton ribs steamed on twigs
plommer <u>plum</u>`·muhr	plums
pommes frites pohm friht	French fries [chips]
portvin <u>poort</u>´·veen	port wine
potet pu·<u>teh</u>´t	potato
potetgull pu·<u>teh</u>´t·gewl	potato chips [crisps]
potetkroketter pu·<u>teh</u>´t·krohk·keht·tuhr	potato croquettes
potetmos pu·<u>teh</u>´t·moos	mashed potatoes
potetsalat pu·<u>teh</u>´t·sah·laht	potato salad
purre <u>pewr</u>`·ruh	leeks
pølse <u>purl</u>´·suh	sausage
pære <u>pa</u>`·ruh	pear
pære Belle Helene <u>pa</u>`·ruh behl heh·<u>leh</u>´n	poached pears with vanilla ice cream and chocolate
rabarbra rah·<u>bahr</u>´·brah	rhubarb
rakørret <u>rah</u>`k·urr·ruht	salt-cured and fermented trout
raspeball <u>rahs</u>`·puh·bahl	potato dumplings
reddiker <u>rehd</u>´·dihk·kuhr	radishes
regnbueørret <u>rayn</u>`·b**ew**·uh·urr·ruht	rainbow trout

rekecocktail <u>reh</u>`·kuh·kohk·tayl	shrimp [prawn] cocktail
reker <u>reh</u>`·kuhr	shrimp [prawns]
rips rihps	red currants
ris rees	rice
ristet brød <u>rihs</u>`·tuht brur	toast
rogn rohngn	roe
rognebær <u>rohng</u>`·nuh·bar	rowanberries
rosenkål <u>roo</u>´·suhn·**kawl**	Brussels sprouts
rosiner ru·<u>see</u>´·nuhr	raisins
rundstykke <u>rewn</u>´·stuik·kuh	roll
rødbeter <u>rur</u>´·beh·tuhr	beet [beetroot]
rødkål <u>rur</u>´·kawl	red cabbage
rødspette <u>rur</u>`·speht·tuh	plaice
røkelaks <u>rur</u>`·kuh·lahks	smoked salmon
røye <u>rury</u>`·uh	char
rådyr <u>raw</u>´·duir	roe-deer
rådyrsadel <u>raw</u>´·duir·**sah**·duhl	saddle of venison
rådyrstek <u>raw</u>´·duir·stehk	roast venison
ragu rah·<u>gew</u>´	ragout
rapphøne <u>rahp</u>`·hur·nuh	partridge
reinsdyr <u>rayns</u>´·duir	reindeer
reinsdyrmedaljonger <u>rayns</u>´·duir·meh·**dahl**·yohng·uhr	small, round fillets of reindeer
reinsdyrstek <u>rayns</u>´·duir·stehk	roast reindeer
ribbe <u>rihb</u>`·buh	spareribs
ridderost <u>rihd</u>´·duhr·ust	semi-hard cheese with nutty flavor

riskrem <u>ree's</u>·krehm	creamed rice with red berry sauce
roastbiff <u>rohst</u>'·bihf	broiled steak
rom rum	rum
rosévin roo·<u>seh</u>'·veen	rosé wine
rype <u>rui</u>`·puh	grouse, a mountain bird
rødgrøt med fløte <u>rur</u>`·grurt meh <u>flur</u>`·tuh	berry compote with cream
rødvin <u>rur</u>'·veen	red wine
salat sah·<u>lah</u>'t	salad
salt sahlt	salt
saltkjøttlapskaus <u>sahlt</u>`·khurt·lahps'·kevs	Norwegian stew with diced, salted and boiled pork
salvie sahl·<u>vee</u>`·uh	sage
sardell sar·<u>dehl</u>'	canned anchovy
sardin sar·<u>dee</u>'n	sardine
sei say	pollock
selleri sehl·luhr·<u>ee</u>'	celery
sellerisuppe seh·luh·<u>ree</u>'·sewp·puh	celery soup
sherry <u>sher</u>'·rih	sherry
sik seek	whitefish
sild sihl	herring
sildeball <u>sihl</u>'·luh·bahl	potato dumplings filled with minced salted herring
sitron siht·<u>roo</u>'n	lemon
sitronbrus siht·<u>roo</u>'n·brews	lemonade

sjampinjonger sham·pihn·<u>yohng</u>´·uhr	button mushrooms
sjampinjongsuppe shahm·pihn·<u>yohng</u>´·sewp·puh	button mushroom soup
sjokoladepudding shu·ku·<u>lah</u>`·duh·pewd·dihng	chocolate pudding
sjømat <u>shur</u>`·maht	seafood
sjøørret <u>shur</u>`·urr·ruht	sea trout
sjøtunge <u>shur</u>`·tung·uh	sole
skalldyr <u>skahl</u>`·duir	shellfish
skinke <u>shihng</u>`·kuh	ham
slettvar <u>sleht</u>`·vahr	brill
smør smurr	butter
solbær <u>soo</u>´l·bar	black currants
sopp sohp	mushrooms
sorbett sohr·<u>beht</u>´	sorbet
spinat spih·<u>nah</u>´t	spinach
steinbit <u>stayn</u>`·beet	catfish
stek <u>stehk</u>	roast
stekte poteter <u>stehk</u>`·tuh pu·<u>teh</u>´t·uhr	sautéed potatoes
stikkelsbær <u>stihk</u>´·kuhls·bar	gooseberries
stuede poteter <u>stew</u>`·eh·duh pu·<u>teh</u>´t·uhr	potatoes in a white sauce
stør sturr	sturgeon
størje <u>sturr</u>`·yuh	tuna
sufflé sewf·<u>leh</u>´	soufflé
surkål <u>sew</u>´r·kawl	coleslaw
sursild <u>sew</u>´r·sihl	marinated herring
svinefilet <u>svee</u>`·nuh·fih·<u>leh</u>	fillet of pork

svinekam <u>svee</u>`·nuh·kahm	loin of pork
svinekjøtt <u>svee</u>`·nuh·khurt	pork
svinestek <u>svee</u>`·nuh·stehk	roast pork
svisker <u>svihs</u>`·kuhr	prunes
svor svoor	bacon rind [crackling]
sylte <u>suil</u>`·tuh	head cheese [brawn]
sylteagurk <u>suil</u>`·tuh·ah·gewrk	pickled gherkin
syltetøy <u>suil</u>`·tuh·tury	jam
tartarbiff tahr·<u>tah´r</u>·bihf	steak tartare
T-benstek <u>teh</u>´·behn·stehk	T-bone steak
te teh	tea
terte <u>tehr</u>`·tuh	fruit cake
tilslørte bondepiker <u>tihl</u>´·slurr·tuh <u>bun</u>´·nuh·pee·kuhr	layers of stewed apples, cookie [biscuit] crumbs and whipped cream
timian <u>tee</u>´·mih·ahn	thyme
tomater tu·<u>maht</u>´·uhr	tomatoes
tomatsuppe tu·<u>mah´t</u>·sewp·puh	tomato soup
torsk tohrsk	cod
tranebær <u>trah</u>`·nuh·bar	cranberries
tunfisk <u>tew`n</u>·fihsk	tuna
tunge <u>tung</u>`·uh	tongue
tyttebær <u>tuit</u>`·tuh·bar	lingonberry
tørrfisk <u>turr</u>´·fihsk	stockfish
uer <u>ew</u>`·uhr	rosefish (seafood)
vafler <u>vahf</u>´·luhr	waffles
vaktel <u>vahk</u>´·tuhl	quail

valnøtter <u>vahl</u>`·nurt·tuhr	walnuts
vaniljesaus vah·<u>nihl</u>`·yuh·sevs	vanilla sauce
vannmelon <u>vahn</u>`·meh·<u>loo</u>n	watermelon
varm sjokolade vahrm shu·ku·<u>lah</u>`·duh	hot chocolate
vermut <u>vehr</u>´·mewt	vermouth
villand <u>vihl</u>`·lahn	wild duck
vin veen	wine
vodka <u>vohd</u>´·kah	vodka
whisky <u>vihs</u>´·kih	whisky
wienerschnitzel <u>vee</u>´·nuhr·shniht·suhl	breaded veal cutlet
yoghurt <u>yoo</u>´·gewrt	yogurt
øl url	beer
ørret <u>urr</u>`·ruht	trout
østers <u>urs</u>´·tehrs	oysters
åbor <u>aw</u>`·bohr	perch
ål awl	eel

eople

Talking	*99*
Romance	*104*

Talking

Essential

Hello/Hi!	**Hallo/Hei!** hah-<u>loo</u>´/hay
How are you?	**Hvordan står det til?** v... tihl
Fine, thanks.	**Bare bra, takk.** <u>bah</u>`-ruh ...
Excuse me.	**Unnskyld.** <u>ewn</u>´-shewl
Do you speak English?	**Snakker du engelsk?** <u>snahk</u>`-kuhr dew ehng´-ehlsk
What's your name?	**Hva heter du?** vah <u>heh</u>`-tuhr dew
My name is…	**Jeg heter…** yay <u>heh</u>`-tuhr…
Nice to meet you!	**Hyggelig å treffes!** <u>huig</u>`-guh-lih aw <u>trehf</u>`-fuhs
Where are you from?	**Hvor kommer du fra?** voor <u>kohm</u>`-muhr dew frah
I'm from *the U.S./ the U.K.*	**Jeg er fra *USA/Storbritannia*.** yay ar frah *ew-ehs-<u>ah</u>´/<u>stoo</u>´r-brih-tahn-yah*
What do you do?	**Hva jobber du med?** vah <u>yohb</u>`-buhr dew meh
I work for…	**Jeg jobber for…** yay <u>yohb</u>`-buhr fohr…
I'm a student.	**Jeg er student.** yay ar stew-<u>dehnt</u>´
I'm retired.	**Jeg er pensjonist.** yay ar pang-shu-<u>nihst</u>´
Do you like…?	**Liker du…?** <u>lee</u>´-kuhr dew…
Goodbye.	**Adjø.** ahd-<u>yur</u>´
See you later.	**Vi ses.** vee <u>seh</u>`-uhs

...k English? **Snakker du engelsk?** <u>snahk`</u>·kuhr d**ew** <u>ehng´</u>·uhlsk

...es anyone here speak English? **Er det noen her som snakker engelsk?** <u>ar</u> deh <u>noo`</u>·uhn h**a**r sohm <u>snahk`</u>·kuhr <u>ehng´</u>·uhlsk

I don't speak (much) Norwegian. **Jeg snakker ikke (så bra) norsk.** yay <u>snahk`</u>·kuhr <u>ihk`</u>·kuh (saw br**ah**) norsk

Could you speak more slowly? **Kan du snakke litt langsommere?** kahn d**ew** <u>snahk`</u>·kuh liht <u>lahng`</u>·sohm·muh·ruh

Could you repeat that? **Kan du gjenta det?** kahn d**ew** <u>yehn´</u>·tah deh

Excuse me. **Unnskyld.** <u>ewn´</u>·shewl

What was that? **Hva sa du?** vah s**ah** d**ew**

Can you write it down? **Kan du skrive det?** kahn d**ew** <u>skree`</u>·vuh deh

Can you translate this for me? **Kan du oversette dette for meg?** kahn d**ew** <u>aw`</u>·vuhr·seht·tuh <u>deht`</u>·tuh fohr may

What does this mean? **Hva betyr dette?** vah buh·<u>tui´r</u> <u>deht`</u>·tuh

I (don't) understand. **Jeg forstår (ikke).** yay for·<u>staw´r</u> (<u>ihk`</u>·kuh)

Do you understand? **Forstår du?** for·<u>staw´r</u> d**ew**

You May Hear...

Jeg snakker ikke engelsk. <u>yay snahk`</u>·kuhr <u>ihk`</u>·kuh <u>ehng´</u>·uhlsk | I don't speak English.

Making Friends

Hello/Hi! **Hallo/Hei!** hah·<u>loo´</u>/hay

Good morning. **God morgen.** gum·<u>maw`</u>·ruhn

Good afternoon. **God dag.** gud·<u>dah´g</u>

Good evening. **God aften/God kveld.** gu·<u>ahf´</u>·tuhn/guk·<u>kvehl´</u>

My name is... **Jeg heter...** yay <u>heh`</u>·tuhr...

Can I introduce you to…?	**Kan jeg få presentere deg for…?** kahn yay faw pre·sahng·<u>teh</u>´·ruh day fohr…
Nice to meet you!	**Hyggelig å treffes!** <u>huig</u>`·guh·lih oh <u>trehf</u>´·fuhs
How are you?	**Hvordan står det til?** <u>voor</u>´·dahn <u>stawr</u> deh tihl
Fine, thanks.	**Bare bra, takk.** <u>bah</u>`·ruh brah tahk
And you?	**Og med deg?** oh meh day

De (the formal form of "you") is generally no longer used to address strangers, but is restricted to written works and addressing older people. As a general rule, **du** can be used in all situations without offending anyone.

Travel Talk

I'm here...	**Jeg er her...** yay ar har...
– on business	**– i forretninger** ih fohr·<u>reht´</u>·nihng·uhr
– on vacation [holiday]	**– på ferie** poh <u>feh´r</u>·yuh
– studying	**– som student** sohm stew·<u>dehn´t</u>
I'm staying for...	**Jeg blir her...** yay bleer har...
I've been here...	**Jeg har vært her...** yay ha**hr** vehrt har...
– a day	**– en dag** ehn dahg
– a week	**– en uke** ehn <u>ew`</u>·kuh
– a month	**– en måned** ehn <u>maw`</u>·nuhd

▶ For numbers, see page 163.

| Where are you from? | **Hvor kommer du fra?** voor <u>kohm´</u>-muhr d**ew** frah |
| I'm from... | **Jeg er fra...** yay a**r** frah... |

Relationships

Who are you with?	**Hvem reiser du sammen med?** vehm <u>ray`</u>-suhr d**ew** <u>sahm´</u>-muhn meh
I'm on my own.	**Jeg reiser alene.** yay <u>ray`</u>-suhr ah-<u>leh`</u>-nuh
I'm with...	**Jeg er her med...** yay a**r** har meh...
– my *husband/wife*	**– mannen min/kona mi** <u>mahn´</u>-nuhn mihn/<u>koo`</u>-nah mih
– my *boyfriend/ girlfriend*	**– kjæresten min** <u>kha`</u>-reh-stuhn mihn
– a friend	**– en venn** ehn vehn
– a colleague	**– en kollega** ehn kohl-<u>leh´</u>-gah
When's your birthday?	**Når har du bursdag?** nohr <u>hahr</u> d**ew** <u>bew´rs</u>-d**ah**g

| How old are you? | **Hvor gammel er du?** voor <u>gahm</u>`-muhl ar dew |
| I'm… | **Jeg er…** yay ar… |

▶ For numbers, see page 163.

Are you married?	**Er du gift?** ar dew yihft
I'm…	**Jeg er…** yay ar…
– single	**– ugift** <u>ew</u>`-yihft
– in a relationship	**– opptatt** <u>ohp</u>´-taht
– married	**– gift** yihft
– divorced	**– skilt** shihlt
– separated	**– separert** seh·pah·<u>reh</u>´rt
I'm widowed.	**Jeg er _enkemann_♂ _/enke_♀.** yay ar <u>ehng</u>`-kuh-mahn♂ /<u>ehng</u>`-kuh♀
Do you have _children/ grandchildren_?	**Har du _barn/barnebarn_?** <u>hahr</u> dew _bahrn/ <u>bah</u>`rn·uh·bahrn_

Work and School

What do you do?	**Hva jobber du med?** vah <u>yohb</u>`-buhr dew meh
What are you studying?	**Hva studerer du?** vah stew·<u>deh</u>´-ruhr dew
I'm studying…	**Jeg studerer…** yay stew·<u>deh</u>´-ruhr…
I work _full time/part time_.	**Jeg jobber _fulltid/deltid_.** yay <u>yohb</u>`-bur _<u>fewl</u>´·teed/<u>dehl</u>´·teed_
Who do you work for?	**Hvem jobber du for?** vehm <u>yohb</u>`-buhr dew fohr
I work for…	**Jeg jobber for…** yay <u>yohb</u>`-buhr fohr…
Here's my business card.	**Her er visittkortet mitt.** har ar vihs·<u>iht</u>´·kor·tuh miht

▶ For business travel, see page 140.

Weather

What's the weather forecast?	**Hva sier værmeldingen?** vah <u>see</u>`·uhr <u>var</u>`·mehl·lihng·uhn
What beautiful weather!	**Så fint vær det er!** soh feent <u>var</u> deh ar
What terrible weather!	**For et forferdelig vær!** fohr eht fohr·<u>fehr</u>´·duh·lih var
It's *cool/warm*.	**Det er kjølig/varmt.** deh ar <u>khur</u>´·lih/vahrmt
It's *snowy/icy*.	**Det snør/er kaldt.** deh snurr/ar kahlt
It's rainy.	**Det regner.** deh <u>rayn</u>`·uhr
It's sunny.	**Sola skinner.** <u>soo</u>´·lah <u>shih</u>´·nuhr
Do I need *a jacket/an umbrella*?	**Trenger jeg jakke/paraply?** <u>trehng</u>´·uhr yay <u>yahk</u>`·kuh/pah·rah·<u>plui</u>´

▶ For temperature, see page 169.

Romance

Essential

Would you like to go out for a *drink/meal*?	**Skal vi gå og ta en drink/ut og spise?** skahl vee gaw *oh tah ehn dringk/ewt oh* <u>spee</u>`·suh
What are your plans for *tonight/tomorrow*?	**Hva gjør du i kveld/i morgen?** vah yurr dew *ih kvehl/ih <u>maw</u>*`·ruhn
Can I have your number?	**Kan jeg få nummeret ditt?** kahn yay faw <u>num</u>´·muhr·uh diht
Can I buy you a drink?	**Kan jeg by på en drink?** kahn yay bui poh ehn drihngk
I like you.	**Jeg liker deg.** yay <u>lee</u>´·kuhr day
I love you.	**Jeg elsker deg.** yay <u>ehls</u>`·kuhr day

Making Plans

Would you like to go out for coffee?	**Skal vi gå og ta en kaffe?** skahl vee gaw oh tah ehn <u>kahf´</u>·fuh
What are your plans for…?	**Hva gjør du…?** vah yurr dew…
– tonight	– **i kveld** ih kvehl
– tomorrow	– **i morgen** ih <u>maw</u>`·ruhn
– this weekend	– **i helgen** ih <u>hehl´</u>·guhn
Where would you like to go?	**Hvor vil du dra?** voor vihl dew drah
I'd like to go to…	**Jeg vil gjerne dra til…** yay vihl <u>ya</u>`r·nuh drah tihl…
Do you like…?	**Liker du…?** <u>lee´</u>·kuhr dew…
Can I have your *number/e-mail*?	**Kan jeg få *nummeret ditt/e-postadressen din*?** kahn yay faw <u>num´</u>·muh·ruh diht/ <u>eh</u>`·pohst·ahd·rehs·suhn dihn

▶ For e-mail and phone, see page 45.

Pick-up [Chat-up] Lines

Can I join you?	**Kan jeg slå meg ned her?** kahn yay slaw may nehd har
You're very attractive.	**Du er svært tiltrekkende.** dew ar svart <u>tihl´</u>·trehk·kuhn·uh
Should we go somewhere quieter?	**Skal vi gå til et roligere sted?** skahl vee gaw tihl eht <u>roo`</u>·lih·uh·ruh stehd

Accepting and Rejecting

I'd love to, thanks.	**Takk, det vil jeg gjerne.** tahk deh vihl yay <u>ya`r</u>·nuh
Where should we meet?	**Hvor skal vi møtes?** voor skahl vee <u>mur`</u>·tuhs
Let's meet at *the bar/your hotel*.	**Vi møtes *i baren/på hotellet ditt*.** vee <u>mur`</u>·tuhs ee <u>bah`</u>·ruhn/poh hu·<u>tehl´</u>·luh diht
I'll come by at…	**Jeg henter deg…** yay <u>hehn`</u>·tuhr day…

▶For time, see page 165.

What's your address?	**Hva er adressen din?** vah ar ahd·<u>rehs´</u>·suhn dihn
Thanks, but I'm busy.	**Takk, men jeg er dessverre opptatt.** tahk mehn yay ar dehs·<u>vehr´</u>·ruh ohp·´taht
I'm not interested.	**Jeg er ikke interessert.** yay ar <u>ihk´</u>·kuh ihn·truhs·<u>seh´rt</u>
Leave me alone.	**Vær så snill å la meg være i fred.** var soh snihl oh lah may <u>va`</u>·ruh ih freh
Stop bothering me!	**Slutt å plage meg!** slewt oh <u>plah`</u>·guh may

Getting Physical

Can I *hug/kiss* you?	**Kan jeg *holde rundt/kysse* deg?** kahn yay <u>*hohl*</u>*·luh rewnt/*<u>*khuis*</u>`*·suh* day
Yes.	**Ja.** yah
No.	**Nei.** nay
Stop!	**Stopp!** stohp

Sexual Preferences

Are you gay?	**Er du homofil?** ar dew hu·mu·<u>fee</u>´l
I'm…	**Jeg er…** yay ar…
– heterosexual	– **heterofil** heh·teh·ru·<u>fee</u>´l
– homosexual	– **homofil** hu·mu·<u>fee</u>´l
– bisexual	– **bifil** bih·<u>fee</u>´l
Do you like *men/women*?	**Liker du *menn/kvinner*?** <u>lee</u>´·kuhr dew *mehn/*<u>*kvihn*</u>`*·nuhr*

▼ Fun

▶ **Sightseeing**	*109*
▶ **Shopping**	*113*
▶ **Sports and Leisure**	*129*
▶ **Culture and Nightlife**	*135*

Sightseeing

Essential

Where's the tourist information office?	**Hvor er turistkontoret?** voor ar tew‑<u>rihst</u>‑kun‑**too**‑ruh
What are the main points of interest?	**Hva er de viktigste severdighetene?** vah <u>ar</u> dih **vihk**‑tik‑stuh seh‑<u>vehr</u>‑dih‑heh‑tuh‑nuh
Do you have tours in English?	**Har dere omvisninger på engelsk?** hahr deh`‑ruh <u>ohm</u>‑vihs‑nihng‑uhr poh <u>ehng</u>‑uhlsk
Can I have a *map/ guide*?	**Kan jeg få *et kart/en guide*?** kahn yay faw *eht kahrt/ehn gied*

Tourist Information Office

Do you have any information on…?	**Har dere informasjon om…?** hahr deh`‑ruh ihn‑fohr‑mah‑<u>shoo</u>´n ohm…
Can you recommend…?	**Kan dere anbefale…?** kahn <u>deh</u>`‑ruh <u>ahn</u>´‑buh‑**fah**‑luh…
– a boat trip	– **en båttur** ehn <u>bawt</u>`‑tewr
– an excursion	– **en utflukt** ehn <u>ew</u>`t‑flewkt
– sightseeing tour	– **en sightseeingtur** ehn <u>siet</u>´‑see‑ihng‑tewr

 Tourist offices are located throughout Norway. The local tourist office can provide information for visitors on accommodation, activities and other entertainment. Visit Norway, the official website of the Norwegian Tourist Board, can provide information about locations in particular cities.

▶For useful websites, see page 169.

Tours

I'd like to go on the tour to…	**Jeg vil gjerne bli med på turen til…** yay vihl <u>ya`r</u>·nuh blih meh poh <u>tew</u>´·ruhn tihl…
When's the next tour?	**Når går neste tur?** nohr gawr <u>nehs</u>`·tuh tewr
Are there tours in English?	**Fins det turer på engelsk?** fihns deh <u>tew</u>`r·uhr poh <u>ehng</u>´·uhlsk
Is there *an English-speaking guide/an audio guide in English*?	**Fins det *en engelsktalende guide/en lydguide på engelsk*?** fihns deh *ehn ehng´·uhlsk·tahl·uhn·uh gied/ehn <u>luid</u>´·gied poh ehng´·uhlsk*
What time do we leave?	**Når drar vi?** nohr drahr vee
What time do we return?	**Når kommer vi tilbake?** nohr <u>kohm</u>´·muhr vee tihl·<u>bah</u>`·kuh
We'd like to see…	**Vi vil gjerne se på…** vee vihl <u>ya`r</u>·nuh seh poh…
Can we stop here…?	**Kan vi stoppe her…?** kahn vee <u>stohp</u>`·puh har…
– to take photographs	– **for å ta bilder** fohr oh tah <u>bihl</u>`·duhr
– to buy souvenirs	– **for å kjøpe suvenirer** fohr oh <u>khur</u>`·puh sew·vuh·<u>nee</u>´r·uhr
– to use the restroom [toilet]	– **for å gå på toalettet** forh oh gaw poh tu·ah·<u>leh</u>´·tuh
Is there access for the disabled?	**Er det adkomst for bevegelseshemmede?** ar deh <u>ahd</u>`·kohmst fohr buh·<u>veh</u>´·guhl·suhs·hem·muhd·uh

▶ For ticketing, see page 19.

Sights

Where *is/are*...?	Hvor er...? voor ar...
– the battleground	– **slagstedet** <u>slah</u>`g·steh·duh
– the botanical gardens	– **den botaniske hagen** dehn bu·<u>tah</u>´·nihsk·uh <u>hah</u>`·guhn
– the castle	– **slottet** <u>slot</u>´·tuh
– the downtown area	– **sentrum** <u>sehn</u>´·trewm
– the fair	– **markedet** <u>mahr</u>`·kehd·uh
– the fortress	– **festningen** <u>fehst</u>`·nihng·uhn
– the fountain	– **fontenen** fon·<u>teh</u>`·nuhn
– the library	– **biblioteket** bihb·lyu·<u>teh</u>´·kuh
– the market	– **torget** <u>tohr</u>´·guh
– the museum	– **museet** mew·<u>seh</u>´·uh
– the old town	– **gamlebyen** <u>gahm</u>`·luh·bui·uhn
– the palace	– **slottet** <u>slot</u>´·tuh
– the park	– **parken** <u>pahr</u>´·kuhn
– the ruins	– **ruinene** rew·<u>ee</u>´n·uh·nuh
– the shopping area	– **handlestrøket** <u>hahn</u>`d·luh·strur·kuh
– the town square	– **rådhusplassen** <u>rawd</u>`·hews·<u>plah</u>·suhn
Can you show me on the map?	**Kan du vise meg på kartet hvor jeg er?** kahn d<u>ew</u> <u>vee</u>`·suh may paw <u>kahr</u>´·tuh voor yay ar

▶ For directions, see page 32.

Impressions

It's…	**Det er…** deh ar…
– amazing	– **praktfullt** <u>prahkt</u>`·fewlt
– beautiful	– **vakkert** <u>vahk</u>´·kuhrt
– boring	– **kjedelig** <u>kheh</u>`·duh·lih
– interesting	– **interessant** ihn·tuh·rehs·<u>sahng</u>´t
– magnificent	– **storslagent** <u>stoo</u>`r·slahg·uhnt
– romantic	– **romantisk** ru·<u>mahn</u>´·tihsk
– strange	– **underlig** <u>ewn</u>`·dur·lih
– stunning	– **overveldende** <u>aw</u>`·vuhr·vehl·duhn·uh
– terrible	– **forferdelig** fohr·<u>fa</u>´r·duh·lih
– ugly	– **stygt** stuikt
I (don't) like it.	**Jeg liker det (ikke).** yay <u>lee</u>´·kuhr deh (<u>ihk</u>`·kuh)

Religion

Where's…?	**Hvor er…?** voor ar…
– the cathedral	– **domkirken** <u>dohm</u>´·khihr·kuhn
– the church	– **kirken** <u>khihr</u>`·kuhn
– the mosque	– **moskéen** mus·<u>keh</u>´·uhn
– the synagogue	– **synagogen** sui·nah·<u>goo</u>`·guhn
– the temple	– **templet** <u>tehm</u>´p·luh
What time is *mass/ the service*?	**Når begynner *messen/gudstjenesten*?** nohr buh·<u>yuin</u>´·nuhr <u>*mehs*</u>`*·suhn/*<u>*gewds*</u>´*·tyeh·nuhs·tuhn*

Shopping

Essential

Where is the *market/ mall [shopping centre]*?	**Hvor er *torget/kjøpesenteret*?** voor ar <u>*tohr*</u>´*·guh/*<u>*khur*</u>´*·puh·sehn·truh*
I'm just looking.	**Jeg bare ser meg omkring.** yay <u>bah</u>`·ruh sehr may ohm·<u>krihng</u>´
Can you help me?	**Kan du hjelpe meg?** kahn dew <u>yehl</u>`·puh may
I'm being helped.	**Jeg får hjelp.** yay fawr yehlp
How much?	**Hvor mye koster det?** voor <u>mew</u>`·uh <u>kohs</u>`·tuhr deh
That one.	**Den der.** dehn dar
No, thanks. That's all.	**Nei takk. Det var alt.** nay tahk deh vahr ahlt
Where do I pay?	**Hvor betaler man?** voor buh·<u>tah</u>´·luhr mahn
I'll pay *in cash/by credit card*.	**Jeg betaler *kontant/med kredittkort*.** yay buh·<u>tah</u>´·luhr *kun·*<u>*tahn*</u>*´t/meh kreh·*<u>*diht*</u>´*·kohrt*
Could I have a receipt?	**Kan jeg få kvittering?** kahn yay faw kviht·<u>teh</u>´·rihng

Norway offers shopping choices for a range of budgets. Even in the capital, a good deal of shopping can be done on foot. Many of the major stores are located in the area around **Karl Johans** gate and on **Bogstadveien** and **Hegdehaugsveien** streets. **Grünerløkka** is the place to go to find trendy boutiques showcasing the work of young Norwegian designers. Here you'll also find lots of second-hand shops, music stores and independent stores selling local pottery and handicrafts.
For everything under one roof in Oslo, visit **Aker Brygge**, **Byporten**, **Glasmagasinet**, **Oslo City**, **Paleet**, **Steen & Strøm** and **Vikaterrassen**.

Regular store hours are Monday to Friday from 9 a.m. to 5 p.m. (on Saturday to 3 p.m.), but many stores stay open later. Shopping malls are generally open Monday to Friday from 10 a.m. to 9 p.m. and Saturday from 9 a.m. to 6 p.m. Most stores are closed on Sunday.

Stores

Where is...?	**Hvor er det...?** voor ar deh...
– the antiques store	– **en antikvitetshandel** ehn ahn·tih·kvih·**teh´ts**·hahn·duhl
– the bakery	– **et bakeri** eht bah·kuhr·**ee´**
– the bank	– **en bank** ehn bahngk
– the bookstore	– **en bokhandel** ehn <u>book</u>`·hahn·duhl
– the clothing store	– **en klesbutikk** ehn <u>kleh</u>`s·bew·tihk
– the delicatessen	– **en delikatesseforretning** ehn deh·lih·kah·<u>tehs</u>´·suh·fohr·reht·nihng
– the department store	– **et stormagasin** eht <u>stoor</u>`·mah·gah·seen
– the gift shop	– **en gavebutikk** ehn <u>gah</u>`·vuh·bew·tihk
– the health food store	– **en helsekostbutikk** ehn <u>hehl</u>`·suh·kohst·fohr·reht·nihng
– the jeweler	– **en gullsmed** ehn <u>gewl</u>`·smeh
– the liquor store [off-licence]	– **et vinmonopol** eht <u>vee</u>`n·mu·nu·pool
– the market	– **et torg** eht <u>tohrg</u>
– the pastry shop	– **et konditori** eht kun·dih·tu·<u>ree</u>´
– the pharmacy [chemist]	– **et apotek** eht ah·pu·<u>teh</u>´k
– the produce [grocery] store	– **en matvarebutikk** ehn <u>mah</u>`t·<u>vah</u>·ruh·bew·tihk
– the shoe store	– **en skoforretning** ehn <u>skoo</u>´·fohr·<u>reht</u>´·nihng
– the shopping mall	– **et butikksenter** eht bew·<u>tihk</u>´·sehn·tuhr
– the souvenir store	– **en suvenirbutikk** ehn sew·vuh·<u>nee</u>´r·bew·tihk

Where is...?	**Hvor er det...?** voor ar deh...
– the supermarket	**– et supermarked** eht <u>sew</u>`·puhr·mahr·kuhd
– the tobacconist	**– en tobakksbutikk** ehn tu·<u>bahk's</u>·bew·tihk
– the toy store	**– en leketøysbutikk** ehn <u>leh</u>`·kuh·turys·bew·tihk

Services

Can you recommend...?	**Kan du anbefale...?** kahn dew <u>ahn</u>`·buh·fah·luh...
– a barber	**– en herrefrisør** ehn <u>hehr</u>`·ruh·frih·surr
– a dry cleaner	**– et renseri** eht rehn·suh·ree´
– a hairdresser	**– en frisørsalong** ehn frih·<u>sur'r</u>·sah·lohng
– a laundromat [launderette]	**– et vaskeri** eht vahs·kuh·ree´
– a nail salon	**– en neglesalong** ehn <u>nay</u>`·luh·sah·lohng
– a spa	**– et spa** eht spah
– a travel agency	**– et reisebyrå** eht <u>ray</u>`·suh·bui·raw
Can you... this?	**Kan du...*denne/dette**?** kahn dew... <u>dehn</u>`·nuh/<u>deht</u>`·tuh
– alter	**– sy om** sui ohm
– clean	**– rense** <u>rehn</u>`·suh
– mend	**– lappe** <u>lah</u>`·puh
– press	**– presse** <u>prehs</u>`·suh
When will it be ready?	**Når er *den/det*** ferdig?** nohr ar *dehn/deh* <u>fa'r</u>·dih

---

* For usage of **denne** and **dette**, see page 162.

** For usage of **den** and **det**, see page 162.

Spa

I'd like...	**Jeg vil gjerne ha...** yay vihl <u>ya</u>`r·nuh h**ah**...
– an *eyebrow/bikini* wax	– **voksing av øyenbrynene/bikinilinjen** <u>vohk</u>`·sihng ah <u>ury</u>`·uhn·bruin·uh·nuh/ bih·<u>kee</u>´·nih·lihn·yuhn
– a facial	– **en ansiktsbehandling** ehn <u>ahn</u>`·sihkts·buh·hahnd·lihng
– a *manicure/pedicure*	– **manikyr/fotpleie** mah·nih·<u>kui</u>`r/<u>foot</u>`·play·uh
– a massage	– **massasje** mahs·<u>sah</u>`·shuh
Do you do...?	**Tilbyr dere...?** tihl´·buir <u>deh</u>`·ruh...
– acupuncture	– **akupunktur** ah·kew·pewngk·<u>tew</u>´r
– aromatherapy	– **aromaterapi** ah·<u>roo</u>´·mah·teh·rah·pee
– oxygen treatment	– **surstoffbehandling** <u>sew</u>`r·stohf·buh·hahnd·lihng
Is there a sauna?	**Fins det sauna?** fihns deh <u>sev</u>´·nah

Many luxury hotels in Norway offer spa and other health and beauty treatments. Geilo is a popular health and wellness retreat where you can also enjoy excellent skiing.

Hair Salon

I'd like...	**Jeg vil gjerne ha...** yay vihl <u>ya</u>`r·nuh h**ah**...
– an appointment for *today/tomorrow*	– **en time *i dag/i morgen*** ehn <u>tee</u>`·muh *ih* d**ah**g/ih <u>maw</u>`·ruhn
– some color	– **litt farge** liht <u>fahr</u>`·guh
– some highlights	– **noen striper** <u>noo</u>`·uhn <u>stree</u>`·puhr
– my hair styled	– **håret stylet** <u>haw</u>´·ruh <u>stiel</u>´·uht
– a hair cut	– **en klipp** ehn klihp
– a trim	– **en stuss** ehn stews

| Don't cut it too short. | **Klipp det ikke for kort.** klip deh <u>ihk</u>`·kuh fohr kohrt |
| Shorter here. | **Kortere her.** <u>kohr</u>`·tuhr·uh har |

Sales Help

When does...*open/ close*?	**Når *åpner/stenger*...?** nohr <u>*aw*`p</u>·nuhr/ <u>stehng</u>`·uhr...
Where is...?	**Hvor er...?** voor ar...
– the cash desk	**– kassen** <u>kahs</u>`·suhn
– the escalator	**– rulletrappen** <u>rewl</u>`·luh·trahp·puhn
– the elevator [lift]	**– heisen** <u>hay</u>´·suhn
– the fitting room	**– prøverommet** <u>prur</u>`·vuh·rum·muh
– the store directory [guide]	**– butikkguiden** bew·<u>tihk</u>´·gie·duhn
Can you help me?	**Kan du hjelpe meg?** kahn dew <u>yehl</u>`·puh may
I'm just looking.	**Jeg bare ser meg omkring.** yay <u>bah</u>`·ruh sehr may ohm·<u>krihng</u>´
I'm being helped.	**Jeg får hjelp.** yay fawr yehlp
Do you have anything in...?	**Har du noe i...?** hahr dew <u>noo</u>`·uh ih...
Can you show me...?	**Kan du vise meg...?** kahn dew <u>vee</u>`·suh may...
Can you *ship/wrap* it?	**Kan du *sende den/pakke den inn*?** kahn dew <u>seh</u>`·nuh dehn/<u>pahk</u>`·kuh dehn ihn
How much?	**Hvor mye koster det?** voor <u>mui</u>`·uh <u>kohs</u>`·tuhr deh
That's all.	**Det var alt.** deh var ahlt

▶ For clothing items, see page 125.

▶ For food items, see page 83.

▶ For souvenirs, see page 121.

You May Hear...

Kan jeg hjelpe deg? kahn yay <u>yehl</u>`·puh day	Can I help you?
Et øyeblikk. eht <u>ury</u>`·uh·blihk	One moment.
Hva skal det være? vah skahl deh <u>va</u>`·ruh	What would you like?
Skal det være noe annet? skahl deh <u>va</u>`·ruh <u>noo</u>`·uh <u>ahn</u>`·nuht	Anything else?

Preferences

I'd like something...	**Jeg vil gjerne ha noe...** yay vihl <u>ya</u>`r·nuh hah <u>noo</u>`·uh...
– cheap/expensive	– **billig/dyrt** <u>bihl</u>`·lih/d<u>u</u>irt
– larger/smaller	– **større/mindre** st<u>urr</u>´·ruh/<u>mihn</u>´·druh
– from this region	– **fra dette området** frah <u>deht</u>`·tuh <u>ohm</u>`·<u>raw</u>·duh
Is it real?	**Er den ekte?** ar dehn <u>ehk</u>`·tuh
Could you show me *this/that*?	**Kan du vise meg *den/den der*?** kahn dew <u>vee</u>`·suh may *dehn/dehn dar*

Decisions

It's not quite what I want.	**Det var ikke akkurat det jeg hadde tenkt meg.** deh vahr <u>ihk</u>`·kuh <u>ahk</u>`·kew·raht deh yay <u>hahd</u>`·duh tehngkt may
No, I don't like it.	**Nei, jeg liker det ikke.** nay yay <u>lee</u>´·kuhr deh <u>ihk</u>`·kuh
That's too expensive.	**Det er for dyrt.** deh ar fohr duirt
I'd like to think about it.	**Jeg må tenke på det.** yay moh <u>tehng</u>`·kuh poh deh
I'll take it.	**Jeg tar det.** yay tahr deh

Bargaining

That's too much.	**Det er for mye.**	deh ar fohr <u>mew</u>`·uh
I'll give you…	**Jeg gir deg…**	yay yeer day…
I only have…kroner.	**Jeg har bare…kroner.**	yay hahr <u>bah</u>`·ruh… <u>kroo</u>`·nuhr
Is that your best price?	**Er det ditt siste tilbud?**	ar deh diht <u>sihs</u>`·tuh <u>tihl</u>`·bewd
Can you give me a discount?	**Kan du gi meg avslag?**	kahn dew yee may <u>ahv</u>`·slahg

▶ For numbers, see page 163.

Paying

How much?	**Hvor mye koster det?**	voor <u>mui</u>`·uh <u>kohs</u>`·tuhr deh
I'll pay…	**Jeg betaler…**	yay buh·<u>tah</u>`·luhr…
– in cash	**– kontant**	kun·<u>tahn</u>´t
– by credit card	**– med kredittkort**	meh kreh·<u>diht</u>´·kohrt
– by traveler's check [cheque]	**– med reisesjekk**	meh <u>ray</u>`·suh·shehk
Could I have a receipt?	**Kan jeg få kvittering?**	kahn yay faw kviht·<u>teh</u>´·rihng

Major credit cards are accepted at most hotels, restaurants, large shops, car rental companies and airlines, though not everywhere, particularly in supermarkets and gas stations. It is a good idea to have some cash on hand, just in case. Traveler's checks are a safe alternative to cash, especially if you do not have a credit card.

You May Hear…

Hvordan vil du betale? <u>voor</u>´·dahn vihl d**ew** buh·<u>**tah**</u>´·luh	How are you paying?
Har du mindre sedler? <u>hahr</u> d**ew** <u>mihn</u>´·druh <u>sehd</u>`·luhr	Do you have any smaller change?

Complaints

I'd like…	**Jeg vil gjerne…** yay vihl <u>ya`r</u>·nuh…
– to exchange this	**– bytte dette** <u>buit</u>`·tuh <u>deht</u>`·tuh
– to return this	**– levere dette tilbake** leh·<u>veh</u>´·ruh <u>deht</u>`·tuh tihl·<u>bah</u>`·kuh
– a refund	**– ha pengene tilbake** hah <u>pehng</u>`·uh·nuh tihl·<u>bah</u>`·kuh
– to see the manager	**– snakke med butikksjefen** <u>snahk</u>`·kuh meh buw·<u>tihk</u>´·sh**eh**f·uhn

Souvenirs

(rose-painted) bowl	**(rosemalt) bolle** (<u>roo</u>`·suh·**mahl**t) <u>bohl</u>`·luh
candlestick	**lysestake** <u>lui</u>`·suh·st**ah**·kuh
cardigan (with Norwegian design)	**lusekofte** <u>lew</u>`·suh·kohf·tuh
doll in native costume	**dukke med bunad** <u>dewk</u>`·kuh meh <u>bew</u>`·nahd
drinking horn	**drikkehorn** <u>drihk</u>`·kuh·h**oo**rn
hunting knife	**jaktkniv** <u>yahkt</u>´·kn**ee**v
plate	**asjett** ah·<u>sheht</u>´
reindeer skin	**reinsdyrskinn** <u>reins</u>´·d**ui**r·shihn
sealskin slippers	**selskinnstøfler** <u>sehl</u>`·shihns·turf·luhr
troll	**troll** trohl
Viking ship	**vikingskip** <u>vee</u>`·kihng·sh**ee**p

wooden figurine	**trefigur** <u>treh</u>`·fih·gewr
woven runner	**rye** <u>rui</u>`·uh
Something typically Norwegian, please.	**Jeg vil gjerne ha noe typisk norsk.** yei vihl yar`·nuh hah <u>noo</u>`·uh <u>tui</u>´·pihsk norsk
Can I see *this/that*?	**Kan jeg få se på *denne/den der*?** kahn yei foh seh poh <u>dehn</u>`·nuh /dehn dar
It's the one in the *window/display case*.	**Det er den i *vinduet/monteren*.** deh ar dehn ih <u>vihn</u>`·dew·uh/<u>mohn</u>`·tuhr·uhn
I'd like...	**Jeg vil gjerne ha...** yei vihl <u>yar</u>`·nuh hah...
– a battery	**– et batteri** eht baht·tuh·<u>ree</u>´
– a bracelet	**– et armbånd** eht <u>ahrm</u>`·bohn
– a brooch	**– en brosje** ehn <u>broh</u>`·shuh
– earrings	**– et par øreringer** eht pahr <u>ur</u>´·ruh·rihng·uhr
– a necklace	**– et halskjede** eht <u>hahl`s</u>·kheh·duh
– a ring	**– en ring** ehn rihng
– a watch	**– en klokke** ehn <u>klohk</u>`·kuh
– copper	**– kobber** <u>kohb</u>`·buhr
– crystal	**– krystall** krui·<u>stahl</u>´
– diamond	**– diamant** dih·ah·<u>mahnt</u>´
– *white/yellow* gold	**– *hvitt/gult* gull** *viht/gewlt* gewl
– pearl	**– perle** <u>par</u>`·luh
– pewter	**– tinn** tihn
– platinum	**– platina** <u>plah</u>´·tih·nah
– sterling silver	**– sterlingsølv** <u>star</u>´·lihng·surl
Is this real?	**Er den ekte?** ar dehn <u>ehk</u>`·tuh
Can you engrave it?	**Kan du få den gravert?** kahn dew foh dehn grah·<u>vehrt</u>´

 Typical souvenirs from Norway include knit items like sweaters and cardigans, gloves and mittens. Other handcrafted pieces like silver, glassware, pottery and hand-painted wooden objects, such as bowls with rose designs, Norwegian trolls, fjord horses and viking ships abound. Art lovers will find that there are also many art galleries across the country. It is a good idea to get local recommendations on where to buy. Goat and reindeer skins as well as furs are also popular.

Antiques

How old is this?	**Hvor gammel er den?** voor <u>gahm</u>·muhl ar dehn
Do you have anything of the...era?	**Har du noe fra...tiden?** hahr dew <u>noo</u>`·uh fra...<u>tee</u>´·duhn
Will I have problems with customs?	**Tror du jeg kan få problemer i tollen?** troor dew yay kahn faw pru·<u>bleh</u>´·muhr ih <u>tohl</u>´·luhn
Is there a certificate of authenticity?	**Har du et ekthetssertifikat?** hahr dew et <u>ehkt</u>´·<u>heh</u>ts·ser·tih·fih·kat

Clothing

I'd like...	**Jeg vil gjerne...** yay vihl <u>yar</u>`·nuh...
Can I try this on?	**Kan jeg prøve den?** kahn yay <u>prur</u>`·vuh dehn
It doesn't fit.	**Den passer ikke.** dehn <u>pahs</u>`·suhr <u>ihk</u>´·kuh
It's too...	**Den er for...** dehn ar fohr...
– big	**– stor** stoor
– small	**– liten** <u>lee</u>´·tuhn
– short	**– kort** kohrt
– long	**– lang** lahng
Do you have this in size...?	**Har du denne i størrelse...?** hahr dew dehn`·nuh ih <u>sturr</u>´·rehl·suh...
Do you have this... in a *bigger/smaller* size?	**Har du denne... i *større/mindre* størrelse?** hahr dew dehn`·nuh... ih *<u>sturr</u>´·ruh/ <u>mihn</u>´·druh* <u>sturr</u>·rehl·suh

▶For numbers, see page 163.

Color

I'd like something in…   **Jeg vil gjerne ha noe i…** yay vihl <u>yar</u>`·nuh hah <u>noo</u>`·uh ih…

- beige — **beige** behsh
- black — **svart** svahrt
- blue — **blått** bloht
- brown — **brunt** brewnt
- gray — **grått** groht
- green — **grønt** grurnt
- orange — **oransje** u·<u>rahng</u>´·shuh
- pink — **rosa** <u>roo</u>`·sah
- purple — **fiolett** fih·u·<u>leht</u>´
- red — **rødt** rurt
- white — **hvitt** viht
- yellow — **gult** gewlt

Clothes and Accessories

backpack	**en ryggsekk** ehn <u>ruig</u>`·sehk
belt	**et belte** eht <u>behl</u>`·tuh
bikini	**en bikini** ehn bih·<u>kee</u>´·nih
blouse	**en bluse** ehn <u>blew</u>`·suh
bra	**en behå** ehn <u>beh</u>`·haw
briefs [underpants]	**en underbukse** ehn <u>ewn</u>`·uhr·buk·suh
coat	**en frakk**♂**/kåpe**♀ ehn frahk♂ / <u>kaw</u>`·puh ♀
dress	**en kjole** ehn <u>khoo</u>`·luh
hat	**en hatt** ehn haht
jacket	**en jakke** ehn <u>yahk</u>`·kuh
jeans	**en olabukse** ehn <u>oo</u>`·lah·buk·suh

pajamas	**en pyjamas** ehn pui·shah´·mahs
pants [trousers]	**en langbukse** ehn lahng`·buk·suh
panty hose [tights]	**en strømpebukse** ehn strurm`·puh·buk·suh
purse [handbag]	**en håndveske** ehn hohn`·vehs·kuh
raincoat	**en regnfrakk** ehn rayn`·frahk
scarf	**et skjerf** eht shehrf
shirt	**en skjorte** ehn shoor`·tuh
shorts	**et par shorts** eht pahr shawrts
skirt	**et skjørt** eht shurrt
socks	**et par sokker** eht pahr sohk`·kuhr
stockings	**et par strømper** eht pahr strurm`·puhr
suit	**en dress ♂/drakt ♀** ehn drehss ♂/drahkt ♀
sunglasses	**solbriller** soo`l·brihl·luhr
sweater	**en genser** ehn gehn´·suhr
sweat suit	**en treningsdrakt** ehn treh`·nihngs·drahkt
swimming trunks	**en badebukse** ehn bah`·duh·buk·suh
swimsuit	**en badedrakt** ehn bah`·duh·drahkt
T-shirt	**en T-skjorte** ehn teh´·shu·rtuh
tie	**et slips** eht shlips
undershirt	**en trøye** ehn trury·uh

Fabric

I'd like…	**Jeg vil gjerne ha…** yay vihl yar`·nuh hah…
– cotton	**– bomull** bum`·mewl
– denim	**– denim** deh´·nihm
– lace	**– knipling** knihp`·lihng

– leather	– **lær** lar
– linen	– **lin** leen
– silk	– **silke** <u>sihl</u>`·kuh
– wool	– **ull** ewl
Is it machine washable?	**Kan den vaskes i maskin?** kahn dehn <u>vahs</u>`·kuhs ih mah·<u>shee</u>´n

Shoes

I'd like…	**Jeg vil gjerne ha…** yay vihl <u>yar</u>`·nuh h**ah**…
– boots	– **støvler** <u>sturv</u>`·luhr
– flat shoes	– **lavhælte sko** <u>lahv</u>`·hehl·tuh sk**oo**
– high heels	– **sko med høye hæler** sk**oo** meh <u>hury</u>`·uh <u>heh</u>`luhrl
– loafers	– **mokkasiner** muk·kah·<u>see</u>´·nuhr
– sandals	– **sandaler** sahn·<u>dah</u>`·luhr
– shoes	– **sko** sk**oo**
– slippers	– **tøfler** turf`·luhr
– sneakers	– **turnsko** t**ewrn**´·sk**oo**
In size…	**I størrelse…** ih <u>sturr</u>`·rehl·suh…

▶For numbers, see page 163.

Sizes

small	**liten** <u>lee</u>`·tuhn
medium	**mellomstor** <u>mehl</u>`·ohm·st**oor**
large	**stor** st**oor**
extra large	**ekstra stor** <u>ehks</u>´·trah st**oor**

Newsstand and Tobacconist

Do you sell English-language *books/newspapers*?	**Har dere *bøker/aviser* på engelsk?** hahr deh`·ruh *bur´·kuhr/ah·vee´·suhr* poh ehng´·ehlsk
I'd like...	**Jeg vil gjerne ha...** yay vihl yar`·nuh hah...
– candy [sweets]	**– noen godter** noo`·uhn goht`·tuhr
– chewing gum	**– en pakke tyggegummi** ehn pahk`·kuh tuig`·guh·gew·mi
– a chocolate bar	**– en sjokoladeplate** ehn shu·ku·lah`·duh·plah·tuh
– cigars	**– noen sigarer** noo`·uhn sih·gah´·ruhr
– a *pack/carton* of cigarettes	**– en *pakke/kartong* sigaretter** ehn *pahk`·kuh/kahr·tohng´* sih·gah·reht´·tuhr
– a lighter	**– en lighter** ehn lie´·tuhr
– a magazine	**– et blad** eht blah
– matches	**– fyrstikker** fuir´·stihk·kuhr
– a newspaper	**– en avis** ehn ah·vee´s
– a *road/town* map of...	**– et *veikart/bykart* over...** eht vay´·kahrt/buih´·kahrt aw·vuhr...
– stamps	**– noen frimerker** noo`·uhn free´·mehr·kuhr

Photography

I'd like...camera.	**Jeg vil gjerne ha...** yay vihl yar`·nuh hah...
– an automatic	**– et helautomatisk kamera** eht hehl´·ev·tu·mah·tihsk kah´·meh·rah
– a digital	**– et digitalkamera** eht dih·gih·tah´l·kah·meh·rah
– a disposable	**– et engangskamera** eht ehn´·gangs·kah·meh·rah

128

I'd like…	**Jeg vil gjerne ha…** yay vihl <u>yar</u>`·nuh·hah…
– a battery	**– et batteri** eht baht·tuh·<u>ree</u>´
– digital prints	**– papirkopi av digitale bilder** pah·<u>pee</u>´r·ku·pee ah dih·gih·<u>tah</u>´·luh <u>bihl</u>´·duhr
– a memory card	**– en minnebrikke** ehn <u>mihn</u>´·nuh·brihk·kuh
Can I print digital photos here?	**Lager dere papirkopier av digitale bilder?** <u>lah</u>`·guhr <u>deh</u>`·ruh pah·<u>pee</u>´r·ku·pih·uhr ah dih·gih·<u>tah</u>´·luh <u>bihl</u>´·duhr

Sports and Leisure

Essential

When's the game?	**Når går kampen?** nohr gawr <u>kahm</u>´·puhn
Where's…?	**Hvor er…?** voor ar…
– the beach	**– stranden** <u>strahn</u>´·nuhn
– the park	**– parken** <u>pahr</u>´·kuhn
– the swimming pool	**– svømmebassenget** <u>svurm</u>`·muh·bahs·sehng·uh
Is it safe to *swim/ dive* here?	**Er det trygt å *svømme/dykke* her?** ar deh truikt aw <u>*svurm*</u>`·muh/<u>*duik*</u>`·kuh har
Can I rent [hire] golf clubs?	**Kan jeg leie golfkøller?** kahn yay <u>lay</u>`·uh <u>gohlf</u>´·kurl·luhr
How much per hour?	**Hvor mye koster det per time?** voor <u>mui</u>`·uh <u>kohs</u>`·tuhr deh pehr <u>tee</u>`·muh
How far is it to…?	**Hvor langt er det til…?** voor <u>lahngt</u>´ <u>ar</u> deh tihl…
Can you show me on the map?	**Kan du vise meg det på kartet?** kahn dew <u>vee</u>`·suh may deh poh <u>kahr</u>´·tuh

Spectator Sports

When's...?	**Når går...?** nohr g**aw**r…
– the basketball game	– **basketballkampen** <u>bah</u>´·kuht·bahl·kahm·puhn
– the cycling race	– **sykkelløpet** <u>suik</u>´·kuhl·**lur**·puh
– the golf tournament	– **golfturneringen** <u>gohlf</u>´·tewr·neh·rihng·uhn
– the soccer [football] game	– **fotballkampen** <u>foot</u>`·bahl·kahm·puhn
– the tennis match	– **tenniskampen** <u>tehn</u>´·nihs·kahm·puhn
– the volleyball game	– **volleyballkampen** <u>vohl</u>´·lih·bahl·kahm·puhn
Which teams are playing?	**Hvilke lag spiller?** <u>vihl</u>´·kuh l**ah**g <u>spihl</u>·luhr
Where's the stadium?	**Hvor er stadion?** voor ar <u>stah</u>´d·yohn
Where can I place a bet?	**Hvor kan jeg spille på hester?** voor kahn yay <u>spihl</u>`·luh poh <u>hehs</u>`·tuhr

Norwegians are very active people and particularly enjoy outdoor sports. Water sports, such as boating, canoeing and fishing are popular, though skiing and hiking are the primary participant sports. In fact, Norwegians boast 4,000 years of skiing, since skis were originally developed as a means of transportation through the snow. Today, there are many ski resorts across Norway and tourist offices can recommend the nearest one for downhill skiing as well as local ski facilities for cross-country skiing. Hiking can be done almost anywhere, but if you're up for an exhilarating experience, try **brevandringer** (guided glacier walks).

Participating

Where's...?	**Hvor er...?** voor ar...
– the golf course	– **golfbanen** <u>gohlf</u>´·bah·nuh
– the gym	– **trimrommet** <u>trihm</u>´·rum·muh
– the park	– **parken** <u>pahr</u>´·kuhn
– the tennis court	– **tennisbanen** <u>tehn</u>´·nihs·bah·nuhn
How much per...?	**Hva koster det per...?** vah <u>kohs</u>`·tuhr deh pehr...
– day	– **dag** d<u>ah</u>g
– hour	– **time** <u>tee</u>`·muh
– game	– **spill** spihl
– round	– **runde** <u>rewn</u>`·duh
Can I rent [hire]...?	**Kan man leie...?** kahn mahn <u>lay</u>`·uh...
– golf clubs	– **golfkøller** <u>gohlf</u>´·kurl·luhr
– equipment	– **utstyr** <u>ew</u>`t·stuir
– a racket	– **en racket** ehn <u>rehk</u>´·kuht

At the Beach/Pool

Where's the *beach/ pool*?	**Hvor er *stranden/ svømmebassenget*?** voor ar <u>strahn</u>´·nuhn/ <u>svurm</u>`·muh·bah·<u>sehng</u>·uh
Is there...here?	**Fins det...her?** fihns deh...h<u>a</u>r
– a kiddie [paddling] pool	– **et barnebasseng** eht <u>bahr</u>´·nuh·bahs·sehng
– an *indoor/outdoor* pool	– **et *innendørs/utendørs* svømmebasseng** eht <u>ihn</u>`·nuhn·d<u>urrs</u>/ <u>ew</u>`·tuhn·d<u>urrs</u> <u>svurm</u>`·muh·bahs·sehng
– a lifeguard	– **badevakt** <u>bah</u>`·duh·vahkt

131

Is it safe...here?	**Er det trygt...her?** ar deh truikt...har
– to swim	**– å svømme** oh <u>svurm</u>`·muh
– to dive	**– å dykke** oh <u>duik</u>`·kuh
– for children	**– for barn** fohr bahn
I want to rent [hire]...	**Jeg vil gjerne leie...** yay vihl <u>yar</u>`·nuh <u>lay</u>`·uh...
– a deck chair	**– en fluktstol** ehn <u>flewkt</u>′·stool
– diving equipment	**– dykkeutstyr** <u>duik</u>`·kuh·ewt·stuir
– a jet-ski	**– en vannscooter** ehn <u>vahn</u>`·skew·tuhr
– a motorboat	**– en motorboat** ehn <u>moo</u>′·toor·bawt
– a rowboat	**– en robåt** ehn <u>roo</u>′·bawt
– snorkling equipment	**– snorkleutstyr** <u>snohr</u>`k·luh·ewt·stuir
– a surfboard	**– et surfebrett** eht <u>sewr</u>`·fuh·breht
– a towel	**– et håndkle** eht <u>hohng</u>`·kleh
– an umbrella	**– en parasoll** ehn pah·rah·<u>sohl</u>′
– water-skis	**– vannski** <u>vahn</u>`·shee
For...hours.	**For...timer.** fohr...<u>tee</u>`·muhr

▶ For travel with children, see page 142.

On good summer days the temperatures in Norway can be warm enough to sunbathe and swim. There are possibilities for diving, waterskiing and windsurfing along the coast and on Norway's many lakes. White-water rafting and kayaking are an adrenaline-pumping option on the rivers in Oppland, Hedmark and Sør-Trøndelag.

Winter Sports

Can I have a lift pass for *a day/five days*?	**Kan jeg få et heiskort for *én dag/fem dager*?** kahn yay faw eht <u>hays</u>`-kort fohr *ehn dahg/fehm <u>dah</u>`g-uhr*
I'd like to rent [hire]…	**Jeg vil gjerne leie…** yay vihl <u>yar</u>`-nuh <u>lay</u>`-uh…
– boots	**– støvler** <u>sturv</u>`-luhr
– a helmet	**– en hjelm** ehn yehlm
– poles	**– staver** <u>stah</u>`-vuhr
– skis	**– ski** shee
– a snowboard	**– et snøbrett** eht <u>snur</u>`-breht
– snowshoes	**– truger** <u>trew</u>`-guhr
These are too *big/small*.	**Disse er for *store/små*.** <u>dihs</u>`-suh ar fohr <u>stoo</u>´-ruh/smaw
Can I take skiing lessons?	**Kan jeg ta skitimer?** kahn yay tah <u>shee</u>´-tee-muhr
I'm a beginner.	**Jeg er nybegynner.** yay ar <u>nui</u>`-buh-yuin-nuhr
Can I have a trail [piste] map?	**Kan jeg få et løypekart?** kahn yay faw eht <u>lury</u>`-puh-kahrt

133

Given the climate and topography of Norway, many of the sports considered "winter" sports can be practiced almost year-round. Skiing is the most popular participant sport in Norway and it is common to take to the slopes from June to September. Major ski resorts are located in Geilo, Hafjell, Hemsedal, Lillehammer, Norefjell (the closest to Oslo) and Trysil. Other snow-oriented activities include: dog-sledding, ice-fishing, skating, sleigh-riding, snowboarding, snowmobiling and tobogganing.

In the Countryside

Can I have a map of…?	**Kan jeg få et kart over…?** kahn yay faw eht kart <u>aw</u>´·vuhr…
– this region	– **dette området** <u>deht</u>`·tuh <u>ohm</u>`·<u>raw</u>·duh
– the walking routes	– **turstier** <u>tewr</u>´·stee·uhr
– the bike routes	– **sykkelstier** <u>suik</u>´·kuhl·stee·uhr
– the trails	– **skiløypene** <u>shee</u>´·lury·puh·nuh
Is it *an easy/a difficult* trip?	**Er det en *lett/vanskelig* tur?** ar deh ehn *leht/<u>vahn</u>`·skuh·lih* tewr
Is it *far/steep*?	**Er det *langt/bratt*?** ar deh *lahngt/braht*
How far is it to…?	**Hvor langt er det til…?** voor lahngt´ ar deh tihl…
Can you show me on the map?	**Kan du vise meg på kartet?** kahn dew <u>vee</u>`·suh may poh <u>kahr</u>´·tuh
I'm lost.	**Jeg har gått meg bort.** yay hahr goht may bu·rt
Where's…?	**Hvor er…?** voor ar…
– the bridge	– **broen** <u>broo</u>´·uhn
– the cave	– **hulen** <u>hew</u>`·luhn
– the farm	– **gården** <u>gawr</u>´·uhn

– the ferry landing	– **ferjestedet** <u>fer</u>`·yuh·steh·duh
– the field	– **jordet** <u>yoo</u>`·ruh
– the fjord	– **fjorden** <u>fyoo</u>´·ruhn
– the forest	– **skogen** <u>skoo</u>´·guhn
– the glacier	– **breen** <u>breh</u>´·uhn
– the hill	– **bakken** <u>bahk</u>`·kuhn
– the lake	– **innsjøen** <u>ihn</u>`·shur·uhn
– the mountain	– **fjellet** <u>fyehl</u>´·luh
– the nature preserve	– **nasjonalparken** nah·shu·<u>nah</u>´l·par·kuhn
– the overlook	– **utsikten** <u>ew</u>`t·sihk·tuhn
– the park	– **parken** <u>pahr</u>´·kuhn
– the path	– **stien** <u>stee</u>´·uhn
– the peak	– **toppen** <u>tohp</u>´·puhn
– the picnic area	– **turområdet** <u>tewr</u>´·um·**raw**·duh
– the pond	– **dammen** <u>dahm</u>´·muhn
– the river	– **elva** <u>ehl</u>´·vah
– the waterfall	– **fossen** <u>foh</u>´·suhn

Culture and Nightlife

Essential

What is there to do at night?	**Hva kan man gjøre om kvelden?** vah kahn mahn <u>yur</u>`·ruh ohm <u>kvehl</u>´·uhn
Do you have a program of events?	**Har du en oversikt over ting som skjer?** <u>hahr</u> dew ehn <u>aw</u>`·vuhr·sihkt <u>aw</u>´·vuhr tihng sohm sh**ehr**

What's playing at the movies [cinema] tonight?	**Hvilke filmer vises på kino i kveld?** vihl`·kuh fihl`·muhr <u>vee</u>`·suhs poh <u>khee</u>´·nu ih kvehl
Where's...?	**Hvor er...?** voor ar...
– the downtown area	**– sentrum** <u>sehn</u>´·trewm
– the bar	**– baren** <u>bahr</u>´·uhn
– the dance club	**– diskoteket** dihs·ku·<u>teh</u>´·kuh
What's the admission charge?	**Hva koster det å komme inn?** vah <u>kohs</u>`·tuhr deh oh <u>kohm</u>`·muh ihn

Culturally, there is a lot to enjoy in Norway. In summer, many cultural events, including orchestral concerts and operas, are celebrated outdoors. Theater is extremely popular, though most is in Norwegian. Classical ballet is performed at the Oslo Opera House and traditional folk dances can be seen across the country.

If you are interested in the visual arts, the Munch museum, named after the internationally-famous Edvard Munch, in Oslo is popular. The extensive National Museum of Art, Architecture and Design is also in Oslo.

Entertainment

Can you recommend...?	**Kan du anbefale...?** kahn d<u>e</u>w <u>ahn</u>´·buh·<u>fah</u>·luh...
– a concert	**– en konsert** ehn kohn·<u>sehrt</u>´
– a movie	**– en film** ehn fihlm
– an opera	**– en opera** ehn <u>oo</u>´·puh·rah
– a play	**– et teaterstykke** eht teh·<u>ah</u>´·tuhr·stuik·kuh
When does it *start/ end*?	**Når *begynner/slutter* det?** norh buh·<u>yuin</u>´·nuhr/<u>slew</u>´·tuhr deh

What's the dress code?	**Hvordan bør man være kledt?** <u>voor´</u>·dahn burr mahn <u>va`</u>·ruh kleht
I like…	**Jeg liker…** yay <u>lee´</u>·kuhr…
– classical music	**– klassisk musikk** <u>klahs´</u>·sihsk mew·<u>sihk´</u>
– folk music	**– folkemusikk** <u>fohl`</u>·kuh·mew·sihk
– jazz	**– jazz** yahs
– pop music	**– pop** pohp
– rap	**– rap** rehp

▶For ticketing, see page 19.

You May Hear…

| **Vennligst skru av alle mobiltelefoner.** <u>vehn´</u>·lihkst skr**ew ah** <u>ahl`</u>·luh mu·<u>bee´l</u>·tehl·uh·**foo**·nuhr | Turn off your cell [mobile] phones. |

The capital offers endless options for going out in pubs, bars, cafes and nightclubs. What's trendy tends to change frequently, so talk to locals to find out where to go. Many clubs offer live music and attract DJs and musicians from around the world. Oslo also has its own growing jazz scene. All restaurants, bars and nightclubs are smoke-free indoors, though many set up outdoor tables in summer and protection for smokers in the winter. Keep in mind that alcohol is considerably more expensive in Norway than in other countries and many clubs enforce age restrictions.

Nightlife

What is there to do at night?	**Hva kan man gjøre om kvelden?** vah kahn mahn <u>yur</u>`·ruh um <u>kvehl</u>´·uhn
Can you recommend…?	**Kan du anbefale…?** kahn d**ew** <u>ahn</u>´·buh·**fah**·luh…
– a dance club	**– et diskotek** eht dihs·ku·<u>**teh**</u>´k
– a gay club	**– en homseklubb** ehn <u>hum</u>`·suh·klewb
– a nightclub	**– en nattklubb** <u>naht</u>`·klewb
Is there live music?	**Er det levende musikk der?** ar deh <u>leh</u>`·vuhn·uh mew·<u>sihk</u>´ d**a**r
How do I get there?	**Hvordan kommer jeg dit?** <u>voor</u>´·dahn <u>kohm</u>`·muhr yay d**ee**t
What's the admission charge?	**Hva koster det å komme inn?** vah <u>kohs</u>`·tuhr deh oh <u>kohm</u>`·muh ihn
Let's go dancing.	**La oss gå ut og danse.** lah ohs g**aw** **ew**t oh <u>dahn</u>`·suh

▼ *Special Needs*

- ▶ *Business Travel*   **140**
- ▶ *Travel with Children*   **142**
- ▶ *For the Disabled*   **145**

Essential

I'm here on business.	**Jeg er her i forretninger.** yay ar har ih fohr·<u>reht</u>´·ning·uhr
Here's my business card.	**Her har du visittkortet mitt.** har hahr dew vih·<u>siht</u>´·kor·tuh miht
Can I have your card?	**Kan jeg få kortet ditt?** kahn yay faw <u>kor</u>´·tuh diht
I have a meeting with…	**Jeg har et møte med…** yay hahr eht <u>mur</u>`·tuh meh…
Where's…?	**Hvor er…?** voor ar…
– the business center	– **forretningssenteret** fohr·<u>reht</u>´·nihngs·sehn·tuhr·uh
– the convention hall	– **konferansesenteret** kohn·fehr·<u>ahng</u>´·suh·sehn·tuhr·uh
– the meeting room	– **møterommet** <u>mur</u>`·tuh·rum·muh

Business Communication

I'm here to attend…	**Jeg er her for å delta i…** yay ar har fohr aw <u>deh</u>`·l·tah ih…
– a seminar	– **et seminar** eht seh·mih·<u>nah</u>´r
– a conference	– **en konferanse** ehn kohn·fehr·<u>ahng</u>´·suh
– a meeting	– **et møte** eht <u>mur</u>`·te
My name is…	**Jeg heter…** yay <u>heh</u>`·tuhr…
May I introduce my colleague…	**La meg få presentere min kollega…** lah may foh preh·sahng·<u>teh</u>´·ruh mihn kohl·<u>leh</u>´·gah…
Nice to meet you!	**Hyggelig å treffes!** <u>huig</u>`·guh·lih oh <u>trehf</u>`·fuhs
I have *a meeting/an appointment* with…	**Jeg har *et møte/en avtale* med…** yay hahr eht <u>mur</u>`·tuh/ehn <u>ah</u>`v·tah·luh meh…

I'm sorry I'm late.	**Jeg beklager at jeg er sent ute.** yay buh‑<u>klah</u>´‑guhr aht yay ar s**eh**nt **ew**´‑tuh
I need an interpreter.	**Jeg trenger en tolk.** yay <u>trehng</u>´‑uhr ehn tohlk
You can reach me at the…Hotel.	**Du kan nå meg på Hotell…** Dew kahn n**aw** may p**aw** hu‑<u>tehl</u>´…
I'm here until…	**Jeg blir her til…** yay bl**ee**r har tihl…
I need to…	**Jeg trenger å…** yay <u>trehng</u>´‑uhr oh…
– make a call	**– ta en telefon** tah ehn teh‑luh‑<u>foo</u>´n
– make a photocopy	**– ta en kopi** tah ehn ku‑<u>pee</u>´
– send an e-mail	**– sende en e-post** <u>sehn</u>`‑nuh ehn **eh**´‑pohst
– send a fax	**– sende en faks** <u>sehn</u>`‑nuh ehn fahks
– send a package (overnight)	**– sende en pakke (over natten)** <u>sehn</u>`‑nuh ehn <u>pahk</u>`‑kuh (**aw**´‑vuhr <u>naht</u>´‑tuhn)

▶ For internet and communications, see page 45.

> **i** Norwegians tend to get right to business and don't engage in much small talk or socializing. You'll find them to be serious and direct in business dealings and in their manner of speaking in general.
>
> Though titles and surnames are used frequently in introductions, they are usually dropped later. Greetings are accompanied by a handshake.

You May Hear...

Har du en avtale? hahr dew ehn <u>ah`v</u>·tah·luh		Do you have an appointment?
Med hvem? meh vehm		With whom?
Han/Hun **er på et møte.** *hahn/huhn* ar poh eht <u>mur`</u>·tuh		*He/She* is in a meeting.
Et øyeblikk. eht <u>ury`</u>·uh·blihk		One moment.
Her har du en stol. har <u>hahr</u> dew ehn stool		Have a seat.
Vil du ha noe å drikke? vihl dew hah <u>noo`</u>·uh oh <u>drihk`</u>·kuh		Would you like something to drink?
Takk for at du kom. tahk fohr aht dew kohm		Thank you for coming.

Travel with Children

Essential

Is there any discount for children?	**Er det reduksjon for barn?** ar deh reh·dewk·<u>shoo´n</u> fohr bahrn
Can you recommend a babysitter?	**Kan du anbefale en barnevakt?** kahn dew <u>ahn´</u>·buh·<u>fah</u>·luh ehn <u>bahr´</u>·nuh·vahkt

Could we have a *child's seat/ highchair*?	**Kan vi få en *barnestol/babystol*?** kahn vee faw ehn <u>bahr</u>`·nuh·stool/<u>beh</u>`·bih·stool
Where can I change the baby?	**Hvor kan jeg bytte på babyen?** voor kahn yay <u>buit</u>`·tuh poh <u>beh</u>`·bih·uhn

Fun with Kids

Can you recommend something for the kids?	**Kan du anbefale noe for barna?** kahn dew <u>ahn</u>`·buh·fah·luh <u>noo</u>`·uh fohr <u>bahr</u>`·nah
Where's…?	**Hvor er…?** voor ar…
– the amusement park	– **fornøyelsesparken** fohr·<u>nury</u>`·uhl·suhs·pahr·kuhn
– the kiddie [paddling] pool	– **plaskebassenget** <u>plahs</u>`·kuh·bahs·sehng·uh
– the park	– **parken** <u>pahr</u>`·kuhn
– the playground	– **lekeplassen** <u>leh</u>`·kuh·plahs·suhn
– the zoo	– **dyrehagen** <u>dui</u>`·ruh·hah·guhn
Are kids allowed?	**Er det adgang for barn?** ar deh <u>ahd</u>`·gahng fohr bahrn
Is it safe for children?	**Er det trygt for barn?** ar deh truikt fohr bahrn
Is it suitable for… year olds?	**Passer det for…åringer?** <u>pahs</u>`·suhr deh fohr…`·awr·ihng·uhr

▶ For numbers, see page 163.

143

Basic Needs for Kids

Do you have...?	**Har dere...?** hahr deh`·ruh...
– a baby bottle	**– en tåteflaske** ehn taw`·tuh·flahs·kuh
– baby wipes	**– papirkluter** pah·pee´r·klew·tuhr
– a car seat	**– et barnesete** eht bahr`·nuh·seh·tuh
– a children's menu/portion	**– en *barnemeny/barneporsjon*** ehn bahr`·nuh·meh·nui/bahr`·nuh·poor·shoon
– a child's seat/highchair	**– en *barnestol/babystol*** ehn bahr`·nuh·stool/beh´·bih·stool
– a *crib/cot*	**– en *barneseng/sprinkelseng*** ehn bahr`·nuh·sehng/sprihng´·kul·sehng
– diapers [nappies]	**– bleier** blay`·uhr
– formula	**– morsmelkerstatning** moors´·mehlk·ehr·staht·nihng
– a pacifier [soother]	**– en narresmokk** ehn nahr`·ruh·smuk
– a playpen	**– en lekegrind** ehn leh`·kuh·grihn
– a stroller [pushchair]	**– en gåstol** ehn gaw´·stool
Can I breastfeed the baby here?	**Kan jeg amme babyen her?** kahn yay ahm`·uh beh´·bih·uhn har
Where can I change the baby?	**Hvor kan jeg bytte på babyen?** voor kahn yay buit`·tuh poh beh`·bih·uhn

▶ For dining with kids, see page 58.

Babysitting

Can you recommend a reliable babysitter?	**Kan du anbefale en pålitelig barnevakt?** kahn dew ahn´·buh·fah·luh ehn poh·lee´·tuh·lih bahr´·nuh·vahkt
What's the charge?	**Hvor mye koster det?** voor mui`·uh kohs`·tuhr deh
We'll be back by...	**Vi er tilbake klokken...** vee ar tihl·bah`·kuh klohk`·kuhn...

I can be reached at... **Jeg kan nås på...** yay kahn n**aw**s poh...

Health and Emergency

Can you recommend a pediatrician?	**Kan du anbefale en barnelege?** kahn d**ew** ahn´•buh•f**ah**•luh ehn b**ah**r`•nuh•l**eh**•guh
My child is allergic to...	**Barnet mitt er allergisk mot...** b**ah**r´•nuh miht **a**r ah•lehr´•gihsk m**oo**t...
My child is missing.	**Barnet mitt er kommet bort.** b**ah**r´•nuh miht **a**r kohm`•muht boort
Have you seen *a boy/girl*?	**Har du sett en *gutt/jente*?** h**ah**r d**ew** seht ehn *gewt/yehn`•tuh*

▶For food items, see page 83.

▶For police, see page 148.

For the Disabled

Essential

Is there...?	**Er det...?** **a**r deh...
– access for the disabled	**– adkomst for bevegelseshemmede** **ah**d`•kohmst fohr buh•**veh**´•guhl•suhs•hem•muhd•uh
– a wheelchair ramp	**– en rullestolsrampe** ehn rewl`•luh•st**oo**ls•rahm•puh
– a handicapped- [disabled-] accessible toilet	**– et handikaptoalett** eht hehn´•dih•kehp•tu•ah•leht
I need...	**Jeg trenger...** yay trehng´•uhr...
– assistance	**– hjelp** yehlp
– an elevator [lift]	**– en heis** ehn hays
– a ground-floor room	**– et rom i første etasje** eht rum ih furr`•stuh eh•**tah**´•shuh

Getting Help

I'm disabled.	**Jeg er bevegelseshemmet.** yay ar buh·<u>veh</u>´·guhl·suhs·hem·muht
I'm *visually/hearing* impaired.	**Jeg er *synshemmet/hørselshemmet*.** yay ar <u>sui</u>´<u>ns</u>·hehm·muht/<u>hurr</u>´·sehls·hehm·muht
I'm unable to *walk far/use the stairs*.	**Jeg kan ikke *gå langt/bruke trappen*.** yay kahn <u>ihk</u>`·kuh *gaw lahngt/<u>brew</u>`·kuh <u>trahp</u>´·puhn*
Can I bring my wheelchair?	**Kan jeg komme i rullestol?** kahn yay <u>kohm</u>`·muh ih <u>rewl</u>`·luh·stool
Are guide dogs permitted?	**Er det adgang for førerhunder?** ar deh <u>ahd</u>`·gahng fohr <u>fur</u>´·ruhr·hewn·nuhr
Can you help me?	**Kan du hjelpe meg?** kahn dew <u>yehl</u>´·puh may
Can you *open/hold* the door?	**Kan du *åpne/holde* døra?** kahn dew <u>awp</u>`·nuh/<u>hohl</u>´·luh dur´·rah

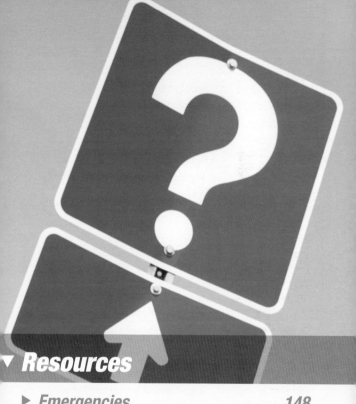

▼ Resources

▶ *Emergencies*		*148*
▶ *Police*		*148*
▶ *Health*		*150*
▶ *Reference*		*158*

Emergencies

Essential

Help!	**Hjelp!** yehlp
Go away!	**Gå vekk!** gaw vehk
Stop, thief!	**Stopp tyven!** stohp <u>tui</u>´·vuhn
Get a doctor!	**Hent en lege!** hehnt ehn <u>leh</u>`·guh
Fire!	**Brann!** brahn
I'm lost.	**Jeg har gått meg bort.** yay hahr goht may boort
Can you help me?	**Kan du hjelpe meg?** kahn dew <u>yehl</u>`·puh may

Police

Essential

Call the police!	**Ring politiet!** ring pu·lih·<u>tee</u>´·uh
Where's the police station?	**Hvor er politistasjonen?** voor ar pu·lih·<u>tee</u>´·stah·shoo·nuhn
There's been an *accident/attack*.	**Det har skjedd *en ulykke/et overfall*.** deh har sh<u>eh</u>d ehn <u>**ew**</u>`·luik·kuh/eht <u>**aw**</u>`·vuhr·fahl
My child is missing.	**Barnet mitt er kommet bort.** <u>bahr</u>`·nuh miht ar <u>kohm</u>`·muht boort
I need...	**Jeg trenger...** yay <u>trehng</u>´·uhr...
– an interpreter	**– en tolk** ehn tohlk
– to contact my lawyer	**– å kontakte advokaten min** oh kun·<u>tahk</u>´·tuh ahd·vu·<u>kah</u>´·tuhn mihn
– to make a phone call	**– å ta en telefon** oh tah ehn teh·luh·<u>foon</u>´

I'm innocent.	**Jeg er uskyldig.** yay ar ew-<u>shuil'</u>-dih

Lost Property and Theft

I want to report...	**Jeg vil anmelde...** yay vihl <u>ahn'</u>-meh-luh...
– a mugging	**– et overfall** eht <u>**aw**`</u>-vuhr-fahl
– a rape	**– en voldtekt** ehn <u>vohl'</u>-tehkt
– a theft	**– et tyveri** eht tui-vuhr-<u>ee'</u>
I've been *robbed/ mugged.*	**Jeg har blitt *ranet/overfalt.*** yay hahr bliht <u>rah`</u>-nuht/<u>**aw**`</u>-vuhr-fahlt
I've lost...	**Jeg har mistet...** yay hahr <u>mihs`</u>-tuht...
...has been stolen.	**...er blitt stjålet.** ...ar bliht <u>styaw'</u>-luht
– My backpack	**– Ryggsekken min** <u>ruig`</u>-sehk-kuhn mihn
– My bicycle	**– Sykkelen min** <u>suik'</u>-kuhl-uhn mihn
– My camera	**– Fotoapparatet mitt** f<u>oo'</u>-tu-ahp-pah-raht-uh miht
– My (rental) car	**– (Leie-)bilen min** (<u>lay`</u>-uh)-<u>b</u>eel-uhn mihn
– My computer	**– PCen min** <u>peh'</u>-seh-uhn mihn
– My credit cards	**– Kredittkortet mitt** kreh-<u>diht'</u>-kor-tuh miht
– My jewelry	**– Smykkene mine** <u>smuik'</u>-kuh-nuh <u>mih`</u>-nuh
– My money	**– Pengene mine** <u>pehng`</u>-uh-nuh <u>mih`</u>-nuh
– My passport	**– Passet mitt** <u>pahs'</u>-suh miht
– My purse [handbag]	**– Håndvesken min** <u>hohn`</u>-vehs-kuhn mihn
– My traveler's checks [cheques]	**– Reisesjekkene mine** <u>ray`</u>-suh-shehk-kuh-nuh <u>mih`</u>-nuh
– My wallet	**– Lommeboken min** <u>lum'</u>-muh-boo-kuhn mihn
I need a police report for my insurance claim.	**Jeg trenger en politirapport til forsikringskravet mitt.** yay <u>trehng'</u>-uhr ehn pu-lih-<u>tee'</u>-rahp-pohrt tihl fohr-<u>sihk'</u>-rihngs-krah-vuh miht

Health

I'm sick [ill].	**Jeg er syk.** yay ar suik
I need an English-speaking doctor.	**Jeg trenger en lege som snakker engelsk.** yay trehng´·uhr ehn <u>leh`</u>·guh sohm <u>snahk´</u>·kuhr <u>ehng´</u>·ehlsk
It hurts here.	**Det gjør vondt her.** deh yurr vunt har
I have a stomachache.	**Jeg har magesmerter.** yay hahr <u>mah`</u>·guh·smer·tuhr

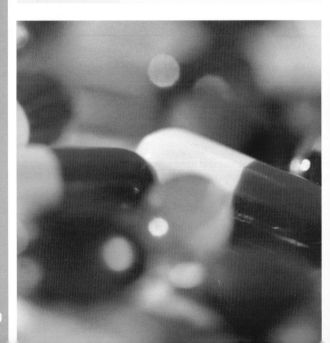

150

Finding a Doctor

Can you recommend a *doctor/dentist*?	**Kan du anbefale en *lege/tannlege*?** kahn dew <u>ahn</u>`-buh-fah-luh ehn *<u>leh</u>`-guh/<u>tahn</u>`-leh-guh*
Can the doctor come to see me here?	**Kan legen komme hit og undersøke meg?** kahn <u>leh</u>`-guhn <u>kohm</u>`-muh heet oh <u>ewn</u>`-nuhr-**sur**-kuh may
I need an English-speaking doctor.	**Jeg trenger en lege som snakker engelsk.** yay trehng´-uhr ehn <u>leh</u>`-guh sohm <u>snahk</u>`-kuhr <u>ehng</u>´-ehlsk
What are the office hours?	**Når er det kontortid?** nawr ar deh kun-<u>toor</u>´-teed
Can I make an appointment...?	**Kan jeg få time...?** kahn yay faw <u>tee</u>`-muh...
– for today	– **i dag** ih d**ah**g
– for tomorrow	– **i morgen** ih <u>maw</u>`-ruhn
– as soon as possible	– **så snart som mulig** soh sn**ah**rt sohm <u>mew</u>`-lih
It's urgent.	**Det haster.** deh <u>hahs</u>`-tuhr

Symptoms

I'm bleeding.	**Jeg blør.** yay bl**u**rr
I'm constipated.	**Jeg har forstoppelse.** yay hahr fohr-<u>stohp</u>´-puhl-suh
I'm dizzy.	**Jeg er svimmel.** yay ar <u>svihm</u>´-muhl
It hurts here.	**Det gjør vondt her.** deh y**u**rr vunt har
I have...	**Jeg har...** yay h**ah**r...
– an allergic reaction	– **fått en allergisk reaksjon** foht ehn ah-<u>ler</u>´-gihsk reh-ahk-<u>shoo</u>´n

I have…	**Jeg har…** yay h**a**hr…
– chest pain	– **vondt i brystet** vunt ih <u>bruis</u>´·tuh
– an earache	– **øreverk** <u>ur</u>´·ruh·vehrk
– a fever	– **feber** <u>feh</u>´·buhr
– pain	– **smerter** <u>smer</u>`·tuhr
– a rash	– **utslett** <u>ew</u>`t·shleht
– sprained…	– **forstuet…** fohr·st<u>ew</u>´·uht…
– some swelling	– **hevelse** <u>heh</u>`·vuhl·suh
– a stomachache	– **magesmerter** <u>mah</u>`·guh·smer·tuhr
– sunstroke	– **fått solstikk** foht <u>soo</u>`l·stihk
I've been sick [ill] for…days.	**Jeg har vært syk i…dager.** yay h**a**hr vert suik ih…<u>dahg</u>`·uhr

▶For numbers, see page 163.

Health Conditions

I have…	**Jeg har…** yay h**a**hr…
– asthma	– **astma** ahst´·mah
– arthritis	– **leddgikt** <u>lehd</u>`·yihkt
– *high/low* blood pressure	– *høyt/lavt* **blodtrykk** huryt/l**a**hvt <u>bloo</u>`·truik
– a heart condition	– **en hjertesykdom** ehn <u>yer</u>`·tuh·suik·dohm
I'm allergic to *antibiotics/penicillin.*	**Jeg er allergisk mot** *antibiotika/penicillin.* yay **a**r ah·<u>ler</u>´·gihsk m**oo**t *ahn·tih·bih·<u>oo</u>´·tih·kah/ peh·nih·sih·<u>leen</u>´*

▶For food items, see page 83.

I'm on…	**Jeg går på…** yay g**a**wr poh…

You May Hear…

Hva er i veien? vah ar ih vay´·uhn — What's wrong?

Er du allergisk mot noe? ar dew ah·ler´·gihsk moot noo`·uh — Are you allergic to anything?

Gap opp. gahp ohp — Open your mouth.

Pust dypt. pewst duipt — Breathe deeply.

Du bør få foretatt en allmenn undersøkelse. dew burr foh faw`·ruh·taht ehn ahl´·mehn ewn`·nuhr·sur·kuh·uhl·suh — I want you to go to the hospital.

Hospital

Please notify my family.	**Vær snill å underrette familien min.** var snihl oh ewn`·nuhr·reht·uh fah·mee´·lyuhn mihn
I am in pain.	**Jeg har smerter.** yay hahr smer´·tuhr
I need a *doctor/nurse*.	**Jeg trenger en *lege/sykepleier*.** yay trehng´·uhr ehn *leh`·guh/sui`·kuh·play·uhr*
What are the visiting hours?	**Når er det besøkstid?** nohr ar deh buh·sur´ks·teed
I'm visiting…	**Jeg skal besøke…** yay skahl buh·sur´k·uh…

Dentist

I've *broken a tooth/lost a filling*.	**Jeg har *brukket en tann/mistet en plombe*.** yay hahr *bruk`·kuht ehn tahn/mihs`·tuht ehn plum`·buh*
I have toothache.	**Jeg har tannpine.** yay hahr tahn`·pee·nuh
Can you repair my dentures?	**Kan du reparere gebisset?** kahn dew reh·pah·reh´·ruh guh·bihs´·suh

Gynecologist

I have *menstrual cramps/a vaginal infection.*	**Jeg har *menstruasjonssmerter/ underlivsbetennelse.*** yay hahr mehn·str**ew**·ah·**shoo**´ns·smer·tuhr/ ewn`·nuhr·**leev**s·buh·tehn·nuhl·suh
I missed my period.	**Jeg har ikke hatt menstruasjon.** yay hahr ihk`·kuh haht mehn·str**ew**·ah·**shoo´n**
I'm on the Pill.	**Jeg tar p-piller.** yay tahr peh´·pil·luhr
I'm (not) pregnant.	**Jeg er (ikke) gravid.** yay ar (ihk`·kuh) grah·**vee**´d
I haven't had a period for…months.	**Jeg har ikke hatt menstruasjon på…måneder.** yay hahr ihk`·kuh haht mehn·str**ew**·ah·**shoo**´n poh…**maw**`·nuhd·uhr

▶ For numbers, see page 163.

Optician

I've lost…	**Jeg har mistet…** yay hahr mihs`·tuht…
– a contact lens	– **en kontaktlinse** ehn kun·tahkt´·lihn·suh
– my glasses	– **brillene mine** brihl´·luh·nuh mih´·nuh
– a lens	– **et brilleglass** eht brihl´·luh·glahs

Payment and Insurance

How much?	**Hvor mye koster det?** voor mui`·uh kohs`·tuhr deh
Can I pay by credit card?	**Kan jeg betale med kredittkort?** kahn yay buh·**tah**´·luh meh kreh·**diht**´·kort
I have insurance.	**Jeg har forsikring.** yay hahr fohr·sihk´·rihng
Can I have a receipt for my health insurance?	**Kan jeg få en kvittering for sykeforsikringen?** kahn yay faw ehn kviht·**teh**´·rihng fohr sui`k·uh·fohr·sihk·rihng·uhn

Where's the nearest pharmacy [chemist's]?	**Hvor er nærmeste apotek?** voor ar <u>ner`</u>·mehs·tuh ah·pu·<u>**teh**</u>´k
What time does the pharmacy [chemist's] *open/close*?	**Når *åpner/stenger* apoteket?** nohr <u>***aw***</u>***`p***·nuhr/<u>*stehng*</u>´·uhr ah·pu·<u>**teh**</u>´k·uh
What would you recommend for…?	**Hva anbefaler du mot…?** vah <u>ahn</u>´·buh·**fah**·luhr dew moot…
How much should I take?	**Hvor mye skal jeg ta?** voor <u>mui</u>`·uh skahl yay tah
Can you fill [make up] this prescription for me?	**Kan du gjøre i stand denne resepten for meg?** kahn dew <u>yur</u>`·ruh ih stahn <u>dehn</u>`·nuh reh·<u>sehp</u>´·tuhn fohr may
I'm allergic to…	**Jeg er allergisk mot…** yay ar ah·<u>ler</u>´·gihsk moot…

Dosage Instructions

How much should I take?	**Hvor mye skal jeg ta?** voor <u>mui</u>`·uh skahl yay tah
How often?	**Hvor ofte?** voor <u>ohf</u>·tuh
I'm taking…	**Jeg tar…** yay tahr…
Are there side effects?	**Er det noen bivirkninger?** <u>ar</u> deh <u>noo</u>`·uhn <u>bee</u>´·vihrk·nihng·uhr

You May See…

EN GANG/TRE GANGER OM DAGEN	*once/three times* a day
DRÅPE	drop
KUN TIL UTVORTES BRUK	for external use only

In Norway, the **apotek** (pharmacy) fills medical prescriptions, while the **parfymeri** (drug store) sells non-prescription items, such as toiletries and cosmetics. Most pharmacies are open during regular business hours: 9 a.m. to 6 p.m. on weekdays. Certain pharmacies may also be open on weekends and a few are open 24 hours a day.

Health Problems

I'd like something for…	**Jeg vil gjerne ha noe mot…** yay vihl <u>yar</u>`·nuh hah <u>noo</u>`·uh moot…
– a cold	– **forkjølelse** fohr·<u>khur</u>′·luhl·suh
– a cough	– **hoste** <u>hus</u>`·tuh
– diarrhea	– **diarré** dih·ah·<u>reh</u>′
– insect bites	– **insektstikk** <u>ihn</u>′·sehkt·stihk
– motion [travel] sickness	– **reisesyke** <u>ray</u>`·suh·sui·kuh
– a sore throat	– **sår hals** sawr hahls
– sunburn	– **solforbrenning** <u>soo</u>`l·fohr·brehn·nihng
– an upset stomach	– **urolig mage** ew·<u>roo</u>′·lih <u>mah</u>`·guh

Basic Needs

I'd like…	**Jeg vil gjerne ha…** yay vihl <u>yar</u>`·nuh hah…
– acetaminophen [paracetamol]	– **paracetamol** pah·rah·seht·tahm·<u>oo</u>′l
– antiseptic cream	– **en antiseptisk salve** ehn ahn·tih·<u>sehp</u>′·tihsk <u>sahl</u>′·vuh
– aspirin	– **aspirin** ahs·pih·<u>ree</u>′n
– a bandage [plaster]	– **plaster** <u>plahs</u>′·tuhr
– a comb	– **en kam** ehn kahm

– condoms	– **kondomer** kun·<u>doo</u>´·muhr
– contact lens solution	– **kontaktlinsevæske** kun·<u>tahkt</u>´·lihn·suh·vehs·kuh
– deodorant	– **en deodorant** ehn deh·u·du·<u>rahnt</u>´
– a hairbrush	– **en hårbørste** ehn <u>haw</u>`r·burr·stuh
– hair spray	– **hårlakk** <u>hawr</u>`·lahk
– ibuprofen	– **ibuprofen** ih·bew·pru·<u>fehn</u>´
– insect repellent	– **et insektmiddel** eht <u>ihn</u>`·sehkt·mihd·duhl
– a nail file	– **en neglefil** ehn <u>nayl</u>`·uh·**feel**
– a *razor/disposable razor*	– **en *barberhøvel/engangshøvel*** ehn bahr·<u>behr</u>´·hurv·vuhl/<u>***ehn***</u>´·gahngs·hurv·vuhl
– razor blades	– **barberblader** bahr·<u>behr</u>´·blah·uhr
– sanitary napkins	– **sanitetsbind** sah·nih·<u>teh</u>´ts·bihn
– shampoo/ conditioner	– **en *sjampo/hårbalsam*** ehn <u>shahm</u>´·pu/<u>haw</u>`r·bahl·sahm
– soap	– **en såpe** ehn saw`·puh
– sunscreen	– **solkrem** <u>soo</u>`l·krehm
– tampons	– **tamponger** tahm·pohng´·uhr
– tissues	– **papirlommetørklær** pah·<u>pee</u>´r·lum·muh·turrk·luhr
– toilet paper	– **toalettpapir** tu·ah·<u>leht</u>´·pah·peer
– a toothbrush	– **en tannbørste** ehn <u>tahn</u>`·burr·stuh
– toothpaste	– **en tannpasta** ehn <u>tahn</u>`·pahst·ah

▶ For baby products, see page 144.

Reference

Grammar

Norway has two official written, mutually comprehensible languages, **bokmål** and **nynorsk**. A traveler in Norway must expect to see and hear both, but **bokmål**—the most common—is used throughout this book.

Verbs

The present tense of regular verbs in Norwegian is formed by adding **-er** to the stem of the verb. The past tense is formed by **-et** or **-te**. The future is formed with **skal** or **vil** + infinitive. This applies to all persons (e.g., I, you, he, she, it, etc.). Following are the present, past and future forms of the verbs **å bytte** (to change) and **å kjøpe** (to buy).

	Present	Past	Future
å bytte (to change)	**bytter**	**byttet**	**skal/vil bytte**
å kjøpe (to buy)	**kjøper**	**kjøpte**	**skal/vil kjøpe**

Irregular Verbs

There are a number of irregular verbs in Norwegian; these must be memorized. Like regular verbs, however, the irregular verb form remains the same, irrespective of person(s). Following are the present, past and future conjugations for a few important, useful irregular verbs.

	Present	Past	Future
å være (to be)	er	var	skal/vil være
å ha (to have)	har	hadde	skal/vil ha
å kunne (to be able to, can)	kan	kunne	skal/vil kunne
å spørre (to ask)	spør	spurte	skal/vil spørre

Imperatives

The imperative is generally the same form as the stem of the verb:

Bytt! Change!   **Kjøp!** Buy!   **Gå!** Go!

Nouns

Nouns in Norwegian can be common (masculine/feminine), feminine or neuter. There are no easy rules for determining the gender. It is best to learn each new word with its accompanying article.

The plural of most nouns is formed by an -(e)r ending (indefinite plural) or an -(e)ne ending (definite plural).

common:	bil**er**	cars	bil**ene**	the cars
neuter:	epl**er**	apples	epl**ene**	the apples

Many monosyllabic nouns have irregular plurals:

en mann	a man	menn	men	mennene	the men
en sko	a shoe	sko	shoes	skoene	the shoes
et hus	a house	hus	houses	husene	the houses
et barn	a child	barn	children	barna	the children

Possession is shown by adding -s (singular and plural). Note that there is no apostrophe.

Johns bror	John's brother
hotellets eier	the owner of the hotel
barnas far	the children's father

Articles

The article (a, an, the) shows the gender of a Norwegian noun, which can be common (masculine/feminine), feminine or neuter. Note that the majority of feminine nouns also have a common form, but usually appear in their feminine form.

1. Indefinite article (a/an)

common:	**en bil**	a car
feminine:	**en** (or **ei**) **jente**	a girl
neuter:	**et eple**	an apple

2. Definite article (the)

Where in English one says "the house", Norwegians tag the definite article onto the end of the noun and say "house-the". In common nouns "the" is **-(e)n**, in feminine nouns, **–a** and in neuter nouns, **-(e)t**.

common:	**bilen**	the car
feminine:	**jenta**	the girl
neuter:	**eplet**	the apple

Personal Pronouns

I	**jeg**
you	**du**
he	**han**
she	**hun**
it	**den/det**
we	**vi**
you (plural)	**dere**
they	**de**

The two forms for "it" refer to the gender. **Den** refers to masculine and feminine nouns, **det** to neuter nouns.

Norwegian has two forms for "you": **du** (informal) and **De** (formal). However, today, the use of the formal **De** has practically disappeared from the language.

Negatives

Negation is expressed by using the adverb **ikke** (not). It is usually placed immediately after the verb in a main clause. In compound tenses, **ikke** appears between the auxiliary and the main verb.

Jeg snakker norsk.	I speak Norwegian.
Jeg snakker ikke norsk.	I do not speak Norwegian.

Questions

Questions are generally formed by reversing the order of the subject and the verb:

Bussen stanser her.	The bus stops here.
Stanser bussen her?	Does the bus stop here?
Jeg kommer i kveld.	I am coming tonight.
Kommer du i kveld?	Are you coming tonight?

Adjectives

An adjective agrees with the noun it modifies in gender and number. For the indefinite form, the neuter is generally formed by adding **-t**, the plural by adding **-e**.

(en) stor hund	(a) big dog	**store hunder**	big dogs
(et) stort hus	(a) big house	**store hus**	big houses

For the definite form of the adjective, add the ending -e (common, neuter and plural). This form is used when the adjective is preceded by **den, det, de** (the definite article used with adjectives) or by a demonstrative or a possessive adjective.

den store hunden	the big dog
de store hundene	the big dogs
det store huset	the big house
de store husene	the big houses

Comparative and Superlative

The comparative and superlative are normally formed either by adding the ending -(e)re and -(e)st, respectively, to the adjective, or by putting **mer** (more) and **mest** (most) before the adjective.

stor/større/størst	big/bigger/biggest
lett/lettere/lettest	easy/easier/easiest
imponerende/mer imponerende/	impressive/more impressive/
mest imponerende	the most impressive

Demonstrative Adjectives

A demonstrative adjective agrees with the noun it modifies in gender and number. If it doesn't refer to a noun, the neuter form is used, e.g., **Hva er det?** What is that?

	common	neuter	plural
this/these	**denne**	**dette**	**disse**
that/those	**den**	**det**	**de**

Adverbs

Adverbs are often formed by adding -t to the corresponding adjective.

rask/raskt	quick/quickly
langsom/langsomt	slow/slowly

Numbers

Essential

0	**null** newl
1	**en** ehn
2	**to** too
3	**tre** treh
4	**fire** <u>fee</u>`·ruh
5	**fem** fehm
6	**seks** sehks
7	**sju** sh**ew**
8	**åtte** <u>oht</u>`·tuh
9	**ni** n**ee**
10	**ti** t**ee**
11	**elleve** <u>ehl</u>`·vuh
12	**tolv** tohl
13	**tretten** <u>treh</u>`t·tuhn
14	**fjorten** <u>fyu</u>`·rtuhn
15	**femten** <u>fehm</u>`·tuhn
16	**seksten** <u>says</u>`·tuhn
17	**sytten** <u>surt</u>`·tuhn
18	**atten** <u>aht</u>`·tuhn
19	**nitten** <u>niht</u>`·tuhn
20	**tjue** kh**ew**`·uh
21	**tjueen** kh**ew**·uh·**eh**´n
22	**tjueto** kh**ew**·uh·<u>too</u>´
30	**tretti** <u>treht</u>`·tih

31	**trettien** treht·tih·**eh**´n
40	**førti** <u>furr</u>´·tih
50	**femti** <u>fehm</u>´·tih
60	**seksti** <u>sehks</u>´·tih
70	**sytti** <u>surt</u>´·tih
80	**åtti** <u>oht</u>´·tih
90	**nitti** <u>niht</u>´·tih
100	**hundre** <u>hewn</u>`·druh
101	**hundreogen** hewn·druh·oh·**eh**´n
200	**to hundre** too <u>hewn</u>`·druh
500	**fem hundre** fehm <u>hewn</u>`·druh
1,000	**tusen** <u>tew</u>´·suhn
10,000	**ti tusen** tee <u>tew</u>´·suhn
1,000,000	**en million** ehn mihl·<u>yoo</u>´n

Ordinal Numbers

first	**første** <u>furr</u>`·stuh
second	**andre** <u>ahn</u>`·druh
third	**tredje** <u>trehd</u>`·yuh
fourth	**fjerde** <u>fya</u>`·ruh
fifth	**femte** <u>fehm</u>´·tuh
once	**en gang** ehn gahng
twice	**to ganger** too <u>gahng</u>`·uhr
three times	**tre ganger** tr**eh** <u>gahng</u>`·uhr

Time

What time is it?	**Hvor mye er klokken?** voor <u>mui</u>`·uh ar <u>klohk</u>`·kuhn
It's noon [midday].	**Den er tolv.** dehn ar tohl
At midnight.	**Ved midnatt.** veh <u>mihd</u>´·naht
From nine o'clock to five o'clock.	**Fra klokken ni til klokken fem.** fra <u>klohk</u>`·kuhn n**ee** tihl <u>klohk</u>`·kuhn fehm
Twenty after [past] four.	**Ti på halv fem.** t**ee** poh hahl fehm
A quarter to nine.	**Kvart på ni.** kvahrt poh n**ee**
5:30 a.m./p.m.	**Fem tretti/Sytten tretti.** fehm <u>treht</u>´·tih/<u>surt</u>`·tuhn <u>treht</u>´·tih
Half past five.	**Halv seks.** hahl sehks

Days

Monday	**mandag** <u>mahn</u>´·dahg
Tuesday	**tirsdag** <u>teers</u>´·dahg
Wednesday	**onsdag** <u>uns</u>´·dahg
Thursday	**torsdag** <u>tawrs</u>´·dahg
Friday	**fredag** <u>freh</u>´·dahg
Saturday	**lørdag** <u>lurr</u>´·dahg
Sunday	**søndag** <u>surn</u>´·dahg

Dates

yesterday	**i går** ih gawr
today	**i dag** ih dahg
tomorrow	**i morgen** ih <u>mawr</u>`·uhn
day	**dag** dahg
week	**uke** <u>ew</u>`·kuh
month	**måned** <u>maw</u>`·nuhd
year	**år** awr

Months

January	**januar** yah·new·**<u>ah</u>´**r
February	**februar** feh·brew·**<u>ah</u>´**r
March	**mars** mahrs
April	**april** ahp·<u>ree</u>´l
May	**mai** mie
June	**juni** <u>yew</u>´·nee

July	**juli** <u>yew</u>´·lee
August	**august** ev·<u>gews´t</u>
September	**september** sehp·<u>tehm´</u>·buhr
October	**oktober** ohk·<u>taw´</u>·buhr
November	**november** nu·<u>vehm´</u>·buhr
December	**desember** deh·<u>sehm´</u>·buhr

Seasons

spring	**vår** vawr
summer	**sommer** <u>sohm`</u>·muhr
fall [autumn]	**høst** hurst
winter	**vinter** <u>vihn´</u>·tuhr

Holidays

January 1	**Første nyttårsdag**	New Year's Day
May 1	**Første mai**	May Day (Labor Day)
May 17	**Syttende mai**	Constitution Day
December 25	**Første juledag**	Christmas Day
December 26	**Annen juledag**	Boxing Day

Movable Dates

	Skjærtorsdag	Maundy Thursday
	Langfredag	Good Friday
	Første påskedag	Easter Sunday
	Annen påskedag	Easter Monday
	Kristi himmelfartsdag	Ascension Day
	Første pinsedag	Whit Sunday
	Annen pinsedag	Whit Monday
	Sankthansaften	St. John's Eve

i

Major holidays in Norway include **Syttende mai** (Constitution Day, May 17), which is celebrated across the country with parades, flags, music, dance and other festivities. **Sankthansaften** (St. John's Eve), Midsummer Night, is the longest night of the year and is also a fun event, traditionally celebrated with bonfires.

Numerous festivals and cultural events are scheduled throughout the year in Norway, some with movable dates. Tourist offices, travel agencies, hotels and guidebooks offer extensive information about local as well as national celebrations. Many festivals are music oriented, featuring folk, chamber, opera and particularly jazz music.

Conversion Tables
Mileage

1 km – 0.62 mi	20 km – 12.4 mi
5 km – 3.10 mi	50 km – 31.0 mi
10 km – 6.20 mi	100 km – 62.0 mi

Measurement

1 gram	**et gram** eht grahm	= 0.035 oz.
1 kilogram (kg)	**et kilogram** eht khee´·lu·grahm	= 2.2 lb
1 liter (l)	**en liter** ehn lee´·tuhr	= 1.06 U.S./0.88 Brit. quarts
1 centimeter (cm)	**en centimeter** ehn sehn´·tih·meh·tuhr	= .4 inch
1 meter (m)	**en meter** ehn meh´·tuhr	= 3.28 feet
1 kilometer (km)	**en kilometer** ehn khee´·lu·meh·tuhr	= 0.62 mile

Temperature

-40° C – -40° F	5° C – 41°F
-30° C – -22° F	10° C – 50° F
-20° C – -4° F	15° C – 59° F
-10° C – 14° F	20° C – 68° F
-5° C – 23° F	25° C – 77° F
-1° C – 30° F	30° C – 86° F
0° C – 32° F	35° C – 95° F

Oven Temperature

100° C – 212° F	177° C – 350° F
121° C – 250° F	204° C – 400° F
149° C – 300° F	260° C – 500° F

Useful Websites

www.visitnorway.com
Official website of the Norwegian Tourist Board

www.visitoslo.com
Oslo Tourist Board

www.visitbergen.com
Bergen Tourist Board

www.sas.dk
Scandinavian Airlines

www.nsb.no
Norwegian State Railways (English available)

www.fjord1.no
Fjord1 Ferry Services (English available)

www.tide.no
Tide Bus and Ferry Services (English available)

www.tsa.gov
U.S. Transportation Security Administration (TSA)

www.caa.co.uk
U.K. Civil Aviation Authority (CAA)

www.hihostels.com
Hostelling International

www.berlitzpublishing.com
Berlitz Publishing website

English–Norwegian Dictionary

A

a (common nouns) en; (neuter nouns) et

access (internet) *v* bruke (internett)

accessories tilbehør

accident ulykke

accommodation innkvartering

account konto

acetaminophen paracetamol

acupuncture akupunktur

adapter adapter

address adresse

admission adgang

after etter

afternoon ettermiddag

air conditioning klimaanlegg

airline flyselskap

airmail luftpost

airport flyplass

aisle midtgang

aisle seat sete ved midtgangen

all alt

allergic allergisk

allergic reaction allergisk reaksjon

allowed tillatt

alter *v* endre

alternate route annen rute

aluminum foil aluminiumsfolie

amazing praktfull

ambulance sykebil

American *adj* amerikansk; *n* amerikaner

amusement park fornøyelsespark

anemic blodfattig

antibiotic antibiotikum

antique antikvitet

antiques store antikvitetshandel

antiseptic cream antiseptisk salve

any noe

adj	adjective	adv	adverb	BE	British English
n	noun	v	verb		

anyone noen
anything noe
apartment leilighet
appetizer forrett
appointment avtale
arcade spillehall
area område
area code retningsnummer
aromatherapy aromaterapi
around (nearby) rundt
arrival ankomst
arrive *v* komme frem
arthritis leddgikt
ask *v* spørre
aspirin aspirin
asthma astma
at ved
ATM minibank
attack overfall
attractive tiltrekkende
automatic *adj* automatisk

B

baby baby
baby bottle tåteflaske
baby wipes papirkluter

babysitter barnevakt
back *adv* (direction) tilbake;
 n (body part) rygg
backpack ryggsekk
bag (carrier) bærepose
baggage [BE] bagasje
baggage claim bagasjemottak
bakery bakeri
bandage bandasje
bank (finance) bank
bar (place) bar
barber herrefrisør
basket (store) handlekurv
basketball basketball
bathroom bad
battery batteri
battleground slagsted
be *v* være
beach strand
beautiful vakker
bed seng
before før
beginner begynner
behind bak
beige beige
belt belte

best best

bicycle sykkel

big stor

bike route sykkelsti

bikini bikini

bill regning

birthday fødselsdag

black svart

bland smakløs

blanket ullteppe

bleed *v* blø

blind blind

blood blod

blood pressure blodtrykk

blouse bluse

blue blå

boat båt

boarding ombordstigning

boarding pass
ombordstigningskort

book bok

bookstore bokhandel

boot støvel

boring kjedelig

botanical gardens botanisk
hage

bother *v* plage

bottle flaske

bottle opener flaskeåpner

bowl (container) bolle

boy gutt

boyfriend kjæreste

bra behå

bracelet armbånd

break down *v* (car) få
motorstopp

breakfast frokost

breathe *v* puste

bridge bro

briefs underbukse

bring *v* (something) ta med

British britisk

broken (bone) brukket;
(out of order) gått i stykker

brooch brosje

broom feiekost

brown brun

bug (insect) insekt

bus buss
bus station busstasjon
bus stop bussholdeplass
business forretning
business card visittkort
business center
  forretningssenter
busy opptatt
but men
buy v kjøpe; (treat) by på

C

cable car n taubane
cafe kafé
call n (phone) samtale;
  v (phone) ringe
camera kamera
camp v campe
campsite n campingplass
can v (be able to) kunne;
  n (container) boks
can opener boksåpner
cancel v annullere
candlestick lysestake

car bil
car hire [BE] bilutleie
car park [BE] parkeringsplass
car rental bilutleie
car seat barnesete
carafe karaffel
card kort
cardigan (Norwegian) lusekofte
carry v bære
carry-on (luggage)
  håndbagasje
cart (shopping) handlevogn;
  (luggage) tralle
carton kartong
cash v løse inn; n kontanter
cashier kasse
castle slott
cathedral domkirke
cave hule
cell phone mobil
certificate of authenticity
  ekthetssertifikat
chair stol
chair lift stolheis

change *v* (alter) endre; (baby)
bytte på; (transport) bytte;
v (money) veksle;
n (money) vekslepenger

cheap billig

check (payment) sjekk;
(restaurant) regning

check in *v* (airport) sjekke inn

check-in desk
innsjekkingsskranke

check out *v* sjekke ut

cheers skål

cheese slicer ostehøvel

chemical toilet kjemisk toalett

chemist [BE] apotek

cheque [BE] sjekk

chest bryst

chest pain vondt i brystet

chewing gum tyggegummi

child barn

children's menu barnemeny

children's portion barneporsjon

church kirke

cigar sigar

cigarette sigarett

cinema [BE] kino

city by

classical music klassisk
musikk

clean *adj* ren; *v* vaske

cleaning supplies
rengjøringsmidler

clear *v* (ATM) slette

cliff klippe

cling film [BE] plastfolie

close *v* stenge

closed stengt

clothing store klesbutikk

coat (man's) frakk;
(woman's) kåpe

coin mynt

cold *adj* kald;
n (illness) forkjølelse

colleague kollega

color farge

comb kam

come *v* komme

computer datamaskin

concert konsert

conditioner (hair) hårbalsam

condom kondom

conference konferanse

confirm v bekrefte

constipation forstoppelse

contact lens kontaktlinse

contact lens solution
  kontaktlinsevæske

convention hall
  konferansesenter

contain v inneholde

control n kontroll

cooking facilities
  kokemuligheter

copper kobber

corkscrew korketrekker

corner hjørne

cost v koste

cot [BE] (child's) sprinkelseng

cotton bomull

cough hoste

country land

country code landkode

countryside land

cover charge inngangspenger

cream (ointment) salve

credit card kredittkort

crib (child's) barneseng

crystal krystall

cup kopp

currency valuta

currency exchange office
  vekslingskontor

customs toll

cut v (with scissors) klippe

cute søt

cycling sykling

cycling race sykkelløp

D

dairy melkeprodukter

damage v skade

dance v danse

dance club diskotek

dark mørk

day dag

deaf døv

deck chair fluktstol

declare v (customs) fortolle

deep dyp

delay forsinkelse

delayed forsinket

delete *v* (computer) slette

delicatessen delikatesseforretning

denim dongeri

dentist tannlege

denture gebiss

deodorant deodorant

department store stormagasin

departure avgang

deposit (down payment) depositum

detergent vaskemiddel

diabetic diabetiker

diamond diamant

diaper bleie

diarrhea diarré

dictionary ordbok

diesel diesel

difficult vanskelig

digital digital

digital camera digitalkamera

digital photo digitalt bilde

digital print papirkopi av et digitalt bilde

dinner middag

direction retning

dirty skitten

disabled bevegelseshemmet

discount rabatt

dish *n* (plate) fat; (food) rett

dish detergent oppvaskmiddel

dishwasher oppvaskmaskin

display case monter

disposable camera engangskamera

disposable razor engangshøvel

dive *v* dykke

diving equipment dykkeutstyr

divorced skilt

dizzy svimmel

do *v* gjøre

doctor lege

dog hund

doll dukke

dollar dollar

domestic innenlands

door dør

double dobbel

double bed dobbeltseng

double room dobbeltrom

down ned

downtown sentrum

drag lift skitrekk

dress kjole

dress code kleskode

drink *v* drikke; *n* drikk

drink menu drikkekart

drive *v* kjøre

driver's license førerkort

driving licence [BE] førerkort

drop (liquid) dråpe

drowsiness søvnighet

dry tørr

dry cleaner renseri

dummy [BE] (baby's)
narresmokk

duty (customs) toll

duty-free tollfri

E

earache øreverk

earring ørering

east øst

easy lett

eat *v* spise

economy class turistklasse

electrical outlet strømuttak

elevator heis

e-mail *n* **(message)** e-post;
v sende e-post

e-mail address e-postadresse

emergency exit nødutgang

empty *adj* tom; *v* tømme

end *n* slutt; *v* slutte

English engelsk

English-speaking
engelsktalende

engrave *v* gravere

enjoy *v* nyte

enter *v* gå inn

equipment utstyr

escalator rulletrapp

e-ticket e-billett

excess luggage overvektig
bagasje

evening kveld

event begivenhet

exchange *v* veksle

exchange rate vekslingskurs

excursion utflukt

excuse *v* unnskylde

exit *n* utgang

expensive dyr

express ekspress

express mail ekspresspost

extension (phone) linje

extra ekstra

extra large ekstra stor

eye øye

eyebrow øyenbryn

F

face ansikt

facial ansiktsbehandling

family familie

fan (appliance) vifte

far langt

farm bondegård

fast hurtig

fax *n* faks; *v* fakse

fax number faksnummer

fee gebyr

feed *v* mate

ferry ferge

ferry landing fergested

fever feber

field jorde

fill (a prescription) *v* gjøre i stand

fill out *v* fylle ut

fill up *v* fylle

filling (tooth) plombe

fine (OK) bra

fire (open) ild; (disaster) brann

fire door branndør

first class første klasse

fit *v* passe

fitting room prøverom

fix *v* reparere

fjord fjord

flight flyavgang

floor etasje

flower blomst

folk music folkemusikk

food mat

foot fot

football [BE] fotball

football game [BE] fotballkamp

for for

forest skog

fork gaffel

form (document) skjema

formula morsmelkerstatning

fountain fontene

free fri

freezer fryser

fresh fersk

friend venn

from fra

frying pan stekepanne

full full

full time heltid

G

game (match) kamp

garbage bag søppelsekk

garden hage

gas (car) bensin

gas station bensinstasjon

gate utgang

get v (find) få tak i

get off v gå av

get to v komme til

gift gave

gift shop gavebutikk

girl jente

girlfriend kjæreste

give v gi

glacier bre

glass (drinking) glass

glasses (optical) briller

go v gå

go away v gå vekk

go out v gå ut

gold gull

golf golf

golf club golfkølle

golf course golfbane

golf tournament golfturnering

good god

good afternoon god dag

good evening god aften

good morning god morgen

good night god natt

goodbye adjø

gram gram

grandchild barnebarn

gray grå

green grønn

greeting hilsen

grocery store dagligvarebutikk

ground floor første etasje

guesthouse pensjonat

guide guide

guide dog førerhund

gym trimrom

H

hair hår

hair salon frisørsalong

hairbrush hårbørste

haircut klipp

hairdresser frisør

hairspray hårlakk

halal halal

half halv

handbag håndveske

handicapped handikappet

hard hard

hat hatt

have v ha

head hode

headache hodepine

health food store
helsekostbutikk

health insurance sykeforsikring

hearing impaired
hørselshemmet

heart hjerte

heart condition hjertesykdom

heat varme

heater varmeovn

heavy tung

heel hæl

hello hallo

helmet hjelm

help n hjelp; v (assist) hjelpe;
(oneself) ta selv

here her

high høy

highchair babystol

highway motorvei

hill høyde

hire n utleie; v leie

hold on v (phone) vente litt

holiday helligdag; [BE] ferie

horse hest

hospital sykehus

hot varm

hotel hotell

hour time

house hus

how hvordan

how far hvor langt

how long hvor lenge

how late hvor sent

how many hvor mange

how much hvor mye

hungry sulten

hurry *n* hastverk

hurt *v* gjøre vondt

husband ektemann

I

I jeg

ibuprofen ibuprofen

icy kaldt

identification legitimasjon

ill [BE] syk

important viktig

impressive imponerende

in i

include *v* inkludere

indoor pool innendørs svømmebasseng

inexpensive rimelig

information informasjon

information desk informasjonsskranke

insect insekt

insect bite insektstikk

insect repellent insektmiddel

insert *v* sette inn

inside inni

instant messenger lynmelder

insurance forsikring

insurance claim forsikringskrav

interesting interessant

international internasjonal

internet internett

internet cafe internettkafé

interpreter tolk

intersection veikryss

introduce *v* (person) presentere

iron (clothing) strykejern

J

jacket jakke

jazz jazz

jeans olabukse

jet-ski vannscooter

jeweler gullsmed

jewelry smykker

join v (go with somebody) bli
med

just (only) bare

K

keep v beholde

key nøkkel

key card nøkkelkort

kiddie pool plaskebasseng

kilo kilo

kilometer kilometer

kiss v kysse

knife kniv

know v (something) vite;
(somebody) kjenne

kosher koscher

krone (Norwegian currency)
krone

L

lace knipling

lactose intolerant
laktoseintolerant

lake innsjø

language språk

large stor

last sist

late sen

later senere

launderette [BE]
selvbetjeningsvaskeri

laundromat
selvbetjeningsvaskeri

laundry (place) vaskeri;
(clothes) vask

laundry facilities
vaskemuligheter

lawyer advokat

leather lær

leave v (depart) dra;
(deposit) legge igjen

leave alone v la være i fred

left (direction) venstre;
(remaining) igjen

lens (for glasses) glass

less mindre

lesson time

letter brev

library bibliotek

life boat livbåt
life jacket flytevest
lifeguard badevakt
lift [BE] (elevator) heis
lift pass heiskort
light *adj* (weight) lett;
  adj (color) lys; *n* lys
light bulb lyspære
lighter lighter
like *v* like
line linje
linen (cloth) lin
liquor store vinmonopol
liter liter
little (some) litt
live *v* (exist) leve; (reside) bo
live music levende musikk
loafers mokkasiner
local lokal
lock lås
log in *v* logge seg inn
log off *v* logge seg av
log on *v* logge seg på
long lang
look *n* titt; *v* se

lose *v* miste
loud (voice) høy
love *v* elske
low lav
luggage bagasje
luggage cart bagasjetralle
luggage locker oppbevaringsboks
luggage trolley [BE] bagasjetralle
lunch lunsj

M

machine maskin
machine washable maskinvaskbar
magazine blad
magnificent storslagen
mail post
mailbox postkasse
make *v* lage
make up (a prescription) [BE] *v* gjøre i stand
mall kjøpesenter
man mann; (gentleman) herre

manager (shop) butikksjef	meter meter
manicure manikyr	microwave mikrobølgeovn
many mange	midday [BE] middag
map kart	midnight midnatt
market marked	mileage kjørelengde
married gift	minute minutt
mass (church) messe	miss v mangle
match (matchstick) fyrstikk;	missing savnet
(sport) kamp	mistake feil
massage massasje	mobile (phone) mobil
may (can) kunne	moment øyeblikk
meal måltid	money penger
mean v bety	month måned
measuring cup målebeger	mop mopp
measuring spoon måleskje	moped moped
medication legemiddel	more mer
medium mellomstor	morning morgen
meet v møtes	mosque moské
meeting møte	motion sickness reisesyke
meeting room møterom	motorcycle motorsykkel
memory card minnebrikke	motorboat motorbåt
mend v lappe	motorway [BE] motorvei
menstrual cramps	mountain fjell
menstruasjonssmerter	mouth munn
menu meny	move v flytte
message beskjed	movie film

movie theater kino

much mye

mug *v* overfalle

mugging overfall

museum museum

music musikk

must (have to) måtte

N

nail (human) negl

nail file neglefil

nail salon neglesalong

name navn

napkin serviett

nature preserve nasjonalpark

nauseous uvel

near nær

nearby i nærheten

necklace halskjede

need *v* trenge

new ny

newspaper avis

next neste

next to ved siden av

night natt

nightclub nattklubb

no nei; (not anything) ikke noe

no one ingen

non-alcoholic alkoholfri

non-carbonated kullsyrefri

non-smoking (area) for
  ikke-røykere

noon middag

north nord

Norway Norge

Norwegian *n* nordmann;
  adj norsk

not ikke

nothing ingenting

notify *v* underrette

novice nybegynner

now nå

number (shoes) nummer;
  (counting) tall

nurse sykepleier

O

off av

off-licence [BE] vinmonopol

office kontor

office hours kontortid

old gammel

on på

once én gang

one en

one-way ticket enveisbillett

only bare

open v åpne; adj åpen

opera opera

opposite midt imot

optician optiker

order v (meal) bestille

other andre

outdoor pool utendørs
svømmebasseng

outlet (electric) stikkontakt

overlook utsikt

overnight natten over

P

p.m. (afternoon) om
ettermiddagen; (evening) om
kvelden

pacifier (baby's) narresmokk

pack v pakke

package pakke

paddling pool [BE]
plaskebasseng

pain smerte

pajamas pyjamas

palace slott

pants langbukse

panty hose strømpebukse

paper papir

paper towel husholdningspapir

paracetamol [BE] paracetamol

park n park; v parkere

parking lot parkeringsplass

part time deltid

pass through v være på
gjennomreise

passport pass

passport control passkontroll

password passord

pastry bakverk

pastry shop konditori

path sti

pay v betale

peak topp

pearl perle

pediatrician barnelege

pedicure fotpleie

pen penn

penicillin penicillin

pensioner pensjonist

per day per dag

per hour per time

per kilometer per kilometer

per night per natt

per week per uke

perfume parfyme

period (menstruation) menstruasjon

permit v tillate

petrol [BE] bensin

petrol station [BE] bensinstasjon

pewter tinn

pharmacy apotek

phone telefon

phone call telefonsamtale

phone card telefonkort

phone number telefonnummer

photo foto

photocopy fotokopi

photograph fotografi

pick up v (person) hente

picnic picnic

picnic area turområde

piece stykke

pill pille; (contraceptive) p-pille

pillow pute

pink rosa

piste [BE] løype

piste map [BE] løypekart

place n (location) sted; (in hostel) plass

plaster [BE] (bandage) plaster

plastic wrap plastfolie

plate tallerken; (dessert) asjett

platform [BE] (station) perrong

play n (theatre) stykke; v spille

playground lekeplass

playing card spillkort

playpen lekegrind

please adv vær så snill

plunger klosettpumpe

pocket lomme

point v peke

point of interest severdighet

poles (ski) staver

police politi

police report politirapport

police station politistasjon

pond dam

pop music popmusikk

portion porsjon

possible mulig

post (mail) [BE] post

postage stamp frimerke

postbox [BE] postkasse

postcard postkort

post office postkontor

pot gryte

pound (British currency) pund

pregnant gravid

premium (gas) super

prepaid calling time ringetid

prescription resept

press v (iron) presse

pressure trykk

price pris

print v skrive ut; n (photo) kopi

problem problem

pronounce v uttale

pronunciation uttale

pull v trekke

purple fiolett

push v (open) skyve

pushchair [BE] gåstol

put v sette

put through sette over

Q

question spørsmål

quick rask

quickly øyeblikkelig

quiet rolig

R

racecourse [BE] travbane

racetrack travbane

racket (sport) racket

railway station [BE]
  jernbanestasjon

rain n regn; v regne

raincoat regnfrakk

rainy regnfull

rap (music) rap

rape voldtekt

rash utslett

rate (exchange) kurs

razor barberhøvel

razor blade barberblad

reach v nå

ready klar

real (genuine) ekte

receipt kvittering

receive v motta

recommend v anbefale

red rød

refrigerator kjøleskap

region område

regular (fuel) normalbensin

reindeer skin reinsdyrskinn

relationship forhold

rent v leie

rental car leiebil

repair v reparere

repeat gjenta

report n rapport; v (a crime) anmelde

reservation bestilling

reserve v bestille

restaurant restaurant

restroom toalett

retired (from work) pensjonert

return v (come back) komme tilbake; (give back) levere tilbake

return ticket [BE] tur-returbillett

right (correct) rett; (direction) høyre

ring (jewelry) ring

river elv

road vei

road map veikart

road sign trafikkskilt

rob rane

romantic romantisk

room rom

room service romservice

round (golf) runde

round-trip ticket tur-returbillett

route rute

rowboat robåt

rubbish [BE] søppel

rubbish bag [BE] søppelsekk

ruin ruin

S

safe adj (free from danger) trygg; n safe

sandals sandaler

sanitary napkin sanitetsbind

saucer skål

sauna badstue

save (computer) lagre

scarf skjerf

schedule (transport) rutetabell

scissors saks

sea sjø

sealskin slippers selskinnstøfler

seat plass

see *v* (watch) se; (meet) treffe; (examine) undersøke

sell *v* selge

seminar seminar

send *v* sende

senior citizen pensjonist

separately hver for seg

separated separert

sentence setning

serve *v* servere

service service; (church) gudstjeneste

shampoo sjampo

should burde

sheet laken

ship *n* skip; *v* sende

shirt skjorte

shoe store skobutikk

shoes sko

shop butikk

shopping area handlestrøk

shopping centre [BE] butikksenter

shopping mall butikksenter

shopping trolley [BE] handlevogn

short kort

shorts shorts

show *v* vise

shower dusj

shrine helligdom

sick (ill) syk

side side

side effect bivirkning

sightseeing sightseeing

sightseeing tour sightseeingtur

sign *v* undertegne

silk silke

silver sølv

single (unmarried) ugift

single room enkeltrom

single ticket [BE] enveisbillett

size (clothes) størrelse;
  (shoes) nummer
ski v gå på ski
skis ski
ski lift skiheis
skirt skjørt
slice skive
slippers tøfler
slow langsom
slowly langsomt
small liten
smoke røyke
smoking (area) for røykere
sneakers turnsko
snorkeling equipment
  snorkleutstyr
snow n snø; v snø
snowboard snøbrett
snowshoes truger
soap såpe
soccer fotball
soccer game fotballkamp
sock sokk
someone noen
something noe
somewhere et eller annet sted

soon snart
sore throat sår hals
sorry v beklage
south sør
souvenir suvenir
souvenir store suvenirbutikk
spa spa
speak v snakke
speciality spesialitet
spoon skje
sports idrett
sports massage
  idrettsmassasje
sprained forstuet
square plass
stadium stadion
stairs trapp
stamp v stemple;
  n (postage) frimerke
start v starte
station stasjon
stay v (remain) bli; (reside) bo
steal v stjele
steep bratt
sterling silver sterlingsølv
stocking strømpe

stolen stjålet

stomach mage

stomachache magesmerte

stop *n* (place) holdeplass;
  v stoppe

store (shop) butikk

store directory butikkguide

stove komfyr

straight ahead rett frem

strange underlig

stream bekk

street gate

stroller gåstol

student student

study *v* studere

stunning overveldende

style *v* (hair) style

subway T-bane

subway station T-banestasjon

suit *n* (man's) dress;
  (woman's) drakt

suitable passende

suitcase koffert

sun sol

sunburn solforbrenning

sunglasses solbriller

sunscreen solkrem

sunstroke solstikk

super (gas) superbensin

supermarket supermarked

surfboard surfebrett

swallow *v* svelge

sweater genser

swelling hevelse

swim *v* svømme

swimming pool
  svømmebasseng

swimming trunks badebukse

swimsuit badedrakt

symbol tegn

synagogue synagoge

T

table bord

tablet (medical) tablett

take *v* ta

tampon tampong

taste *v* smake

tax skatt

taxi drosje

taxi rank [BE] drosjeholdeplass

taxi stand drosjeholdeplass

team lag

teaspoon teskje

tell *v* si

temple (religious) tempel

tennis tennis

tennis court tennisbane

tennis match tenniskamp

tent telt

terminal (airport) terminal

terrible forferdelig

text *n* tekst; *v* (message) tekste

than enn

thank *v* takke

theft tyveri

there (place) der; (direction) dit

these disse

thief tyv

thing ting

think *v* (believe) tro

this denne; dette

those de

throat hals

ticket billett

ticket office billettluke

tights [BE] strømpebukse

time (period) tid; (occasion) gang

timetable [BE] rutetabell

tissue papirlommetørkle

to (direction) til; (time) på

tobacco tobakk

tobacconist tobakkshandel

today i dag

toilet [BE] toalett

toilet paper toalettpapir

tomorrow i morgen

tonight i kveld

too for

tooth tann

toothache tannpine

toothbrush tannbørste

toothpaste tannpasta

tour tur

tourist office turistkontor

towel håndkle

town by

town map bykart
town square torg
toy leketøy
toy store leketøysbutikk
track (railway) spor
traditional tradisjonell
traffic light trafikklys
trail løype
trail map løypekart
train tog
train schedule togtabell
train station jernbanestasjon
tram trikk
translate v oversette
trash søppel
travel v reise
travel agency reisebyrå
travel guide reisehåndbok
travel sickness reisesyke
traveler's check reisesjekk
trim (hair) stuss
trip tur
troll troll
trousers [BE] langbukse
try on v prøve
T-shirt T-skjorte

turn off (device) skru av
turn on (device) skru på
TV TV
type v (computer) skrive
typically typisk

U

ugly stygg
umbrella paraply
underground [BE] n T-bane
underground station [BE]
  T-banestasjon
undershirt trøye
understand v forstå
unleaded blyfri
until til
upset stomach urolig mage
use n bruk; v bruke
username brukernavn

V

vacation ferie
vacuum cleaner støvsuger
vaginal infection
  underlivsbetennelse
valley dal

194

value verdi
VAT [BE] moms
vegetarian vegetarianer
very meget
viking ship vikingskip
visit *n* besøk; *v* (a person) besøke
visiting hours besøkstid
visually impaired synshemmet
volleyball game volleyballkamp
vomit *v* kaste opp

W

wait *v* vente
waiter servitør
waitress servitør
wake *v* vekke
wake-up call vekking
walk *v* (go) gå; (stroll) spasere
wallet lommebok
want *v* ville
warm *adj* varm; *v* varme
wash *v* vaske
washable vaskbar
washing mashine vaskemaskin

watch klokke
water vann
waterfall foss
water skis vannski
weather vær
weather forecast værutsikter
week uke
weekend helg
welcome velkommen
west vest
what hva
wheelchair rullestol
wheelchair ramp rullestolsrampe
when når
where hvor
which hvilken
white hvit
who hvem
whole hel
widowed (man) enkemann; (woman) enke
wife kone
window vindu
window seat vindusplass
windsurfer seilbrett

wine list vinkart

wireless internet trådløst internett

with med

withdraw v (from account) ta ut

without uten

woman kvinne

wooden figurine trefigur

wool ull

work v (toil) arbeide; (function) virke

wrap up v pakke inn

write v skrive

wrong i veien

Y

year år

yellow gul

yes ja

yesterday i går

you du

youth hostel vandrerhjem

Z

zoo dyrehage

Norwegian–English Dictionary

A

adapter adapter
adjø goodbye
adresse address
advokat lawyer
akkurat nå right now
akupunktur acupuncture
alkoholfri non-alcoholic
allergisk allergic
allergisk reaksjon allergic reaction
alt all
aluminiumsfolie aluminum foil
amerikaner *n* American
amerikansk *adj* American
anbefale *v* recommend
andre other
ankomst arrival
anmelde *v* report (a theft)
annen rute alternate route
annullere *v* cancel
ansikt face

ansiktsbehandling facial
antibiotikum antibiotic
antikvitet antique
antikvitetshandel antiques store
antiseptisk salve antiseptic cream
aperitiff aperitif
apotek pharmacy [chemist BE]
arbeide *v* work
armbånd bracelet
aromaterapi aromatherapy
asjett plate (dessert)
aspirin aspirin
astma asthma
automatisk automatic
av off
avgang departure
avis newspaper
avtale appointment

B

baby baby
babystol highchair
bad bathroom

badebukse swimming trunks

badedrakt swimsuit

badevakt lifeguard

badstue sauna

bagasje luggage [baggage BE]

bagasjemottak baggage claim

bagasjetralle luggage cart [trolley BE]

bak behind

bakeri bakery

bakverk pastry

bandasje bandage

bank bank (finance)

bar *n* bar (place)

barberblad razor blade

barberhøvel razor

bare just; only

barn child

barnebarn grandchild

barnelege pediatrician

barnemeny children's menu

barneporsjon children's portion

barnesete car seat

barnevakt babysitter

basketball basketball

batteri battery

be om *v* ask for

begivenhet event

begynner beginner

beholde *v* keep

behå bra

beige beige

bekk stream

beklage *v* be sorry

bekrefte *v* confirm

belte belt

bensin gas [petrol BE] (car)

bensinstasjon gas [petrol BE] station

beskjed message

best best

bestille *v* order (meal); reserve

bestilling reservation

besøk *n* visit

besøke *v* visit (someone)

besøkstid visiting hours

betale *v* pay

bety *v* mean

bevegelseshemmet disabled

bibliotek library

bikini bikini

bil car

billett ticket

billettluke ticket office

billig cheap

bilutleie car rental [hire BE]

bivirkning side effect

blad magazine

bleie diaper

bli *v* stay (remain)

bli med *v* join (someone)

blind blind

blod blood

blodfattig anemic

blodtrykk blood pressure

blomst flower

bluse blouse

blyfri unleaded

blø *v* bleed

blå blue

bo live (reside); stay (reside)

bok book

bokhandel bookstore

boks can (container)

boksåpner can opener

bolle bowl

bomull cotton

bondegård farm

bord table

botanisk hage botanical gardens

bra fine (OK)

brann fire (disaster)

branndør fire door

bratt steep

bre glacier

brev letter

briller glasses

britisk British

bro bridge

brosje brooch

bruk *n* use

bruke *v* use

brukernavn username

brukket broken (bone)

brun brown

bryst chest

burde should

buss bus

bussholdeplass bus stop

busstasjon bus station

butikk store [shop BE]

butikkguide store directory

butikksenter shopping mall [centre BE]

butikksjef manager (shop)

by *n* city; town

bykart town map

bytte *v* change (transportation)

bytte på *v* change (baby)

bære *v* carry

bærepose bag (carrier)

båt boat

C

campe *v* camp

camping camping

campingplass campsite

D

dag day

dagligvarebutikk grocery store

dal valley

dam pond

danse *v* dance

datamaskin computer

delikatesseforretning delicatessen

deltid part time

denne this

deodorant deodorant

depositum deposit (down payment)

der there (place)

dette this

diabetiker diabetic

diamant diamond

diarré diarrhea

die breastfeed

diesel diesel

digital digital

digitalkamera digital camera

digitalt bilde digital photo

diskotek dance club

disse these

dit there (direction)

dobbel double

dobbeltrom double room

dobbeltseng double bed

dollar dollar

domkirke cathedral

dongeri denim

dra *v* leave (depart)

drakt suit (woman's)

dress suit (man's)

drikk *n* drink

drikke *v* drink

drikkekart drink menu

drosje taxi

drosjeholdeplass taxi stand
  [rank BE]

dråpe drop (liquid)

du you

dukke doll

dusj shower

dykke *v* dive

dykkeutstyr diving equipment

dyp *adj* deep

dyr *adj* expensive

dyrehage zoo

dør door

døv deaf

E

e-billett e-ticket

ekspert expert

ekspress express

ekspresspost express mail

ekstra extra

ekstra stor extra large

ekte real (genuine)

ektemann husband

ekthetssertifikat certificate of
  authenticity

elske *v* love

elv river

en a (common nouns); one

endre *v* change

engangshøvel disposable razor

engangskamera disposable
  camera

engelsk English

engelsktalende
  English-speaking

enke widowed (woman)

enkeltrom single room

enkemann widowed (man)

enn than

enveisbillett one-way
  [single BE] ticket

e-post e-mail

e-postadresse e-mail addess

erfaren experienced

et a (neuter nouns)

et eller annet sted somewhere

et øyeblikk hold on (phone)

etasje floor

etter after

ettermiddag afternoon

F

faks *n* fax

fakse *v* fax

faksnummer fax number

familie family

farge color

fat dish

feber fever

feiekost broom

feil mistake

ferge ferry

ferie vacation [holiday BE]

fersk fresh

film movie

fiolett purple

fjell mountain

fjord fjord

flaske bottle

flaskeåpner bottle opener

fluktstol deck chair

fly flight

flyplass airport

flyselskap airline

flytevest life jacket

flytte *v* move

folkemusikk folk music

fontene fountain

for for; too

for røykere smoking (area)

forferdelig terrible

forhold relationship

forkjølelse cold (illness)

fornøyelsespark amusement park

forretning business

forretningssenter business center

forrett appetizer

forsikring insurance

forsikringskrav insurance claim

forsinkelse delay

forsinket delayed

forstoppelse constipation

forstuet sprained

forstå v understand

fortolle v declare (customs)

foss waterfall

fot foot

fotball soccer [football BE]

fotballkamp soccer
 [football BE] game

foto photo

fotokopi photocopy

fotpleie pedicure

fra from

frakk coat (man's)

fri free

frimerke stamp (postage)

frisør hairdresser

frisørsalong hair salon

frokost breakfast

fryser freezer

full full

fylle v fill up

fylle ut v fill out

fyrstikk match (matchstick)

fødselsdag birthday

før before

førerhund guide dog

førerkort driver's license
 [driving licence BE]

første etasje ground floor

første klasse first class

få motorstopp v break down
 (car)

få tak i v get (find)

G

gaffel fork

gammel old

gang time (occasion)

gate street

gave gift

gavebutikk gift shop

gebiss denture

gebyr fee

genser sweater

gi v give

gift adj married

gir n speed (cycle)

gjenta v repeat

gjøre v do

gjøre i stand v make up
 (prepare)

gjøre vondt *v* hurt

glass glass (drinking)

glass lens (for glasses)

god good

god aften good evening

god dag good afternoon

god morgen good morning

god natt good night

godter candy

golf golf

golfbane golf course

golfkølle golf club

golfturnering golf tournament

gram gram

gravere *v* engrave

gravid pregnant

gryte pot

grå gray

grønn green

gudstjeneste service (church)

guide guide

gul *adj* yellow

gull *n* gold

gullsmed jeweler

gult gull yellow gold

gutt boy

gå *v* go; walk

gå av *v* get off

gå inn *v* enter

gå på ski *v* ski

gå seg bort *v* get lost

gå ut *v* go out

gå vekk go away

gåstol stroller [pushchair BE]

gått i stykker broken (out of order)

H

ha *v* have

ha det travelt *v* be in a hurry

ha gått seg bort *v* be lost

hage garden

halal halal

hallo hello

hals throat

halskjede necklace

halv half

halvtime half an hour

handikappet handicapped

handlekurv basket (shopping)

handlestrøk shopping area

handlevogn shopping cart [trolley BE]

hans his

hard hard

haste *v* be urgent

hatt hat

heis elevator [lift BE]

heiskort lift pass

hel whole

helg weekend

helligdag holiday

helligdom shrine

helsekostbutikk health food store

heltid full time

hennes her

hente *v* pick up (person)

her here

herre man (gentleman)

herrefrisør barber

hest horse

hevelse swelling

hilsen greeting

hjelm helmet

hjelp *n* help

hjelpe *v* help

hjerte heart

hjertesykdom heart condition

hjørne corner

hode head

hodepine headache

holde rundt hug

holdeplass stop (place)

hoste *v* cough

hotell hotel

hule *n* cave

hullsleiv spatula

hund dog

hurtig fast

hus house

husholdningspapir paper towel

hva what

hvem who

hver for oss separately

hvilken which

hvit white

hvitt gull white gold

hvor where

hvor langt how far

hvor lenge how long

hvor mange how many

hvor mye how much

hvor sent how late

hvordan how

hæl heel

hørselshemmet hearing impaired

høy high (tall); loud (voice)

høyde hill

høyre right (direction)

håndbagasje carry-on (luggage)

håndkle towel

håndveske handbag

hår hair

hårbalsam conditioner (hair)

hårbørste hairbrush

hårlakk hair spray

I

i in

i dag today

i går yesterday

i kveld tonight

i morgen tomorrow

i nærheten nearby

i veien wrong

ibuprofen ibuprofen

idrett sports

idrettsmassasje sports massage

igjen left (remaining)

ikke not

ikke noe no (not anything)

ild fire (open)

imponerende impressive

informasjon information

informasjonsskranke information desk

ingen no one

ingenting nothing

inkludere v include

inkludert included

inneholde v contain

innendørs svømmebasseng indoor pool

innenlands domestic

inngangsbillett admission (price)

inngangspenger cover charge

inni inside

innkvartering accommodation

innsjekkingsskranke check-in

innsjø lake

insekt insect, bug

insektmiddel insect repellent

insektstikk insect bite

interessant interesting

interessert interested

internasjonal international

internett internet

internettkafé internet cafe

J

ja yes

jakke jacket

jazz jazz

jeg I

jente girl

jernbanestasjon train
  [railway BE] station

jorde field

K

kafé cafe

kald cold

kaldt icy

kam comb

kamera camera

kamp game; match (sport)

karaffel carafe

kart map

kartong carton

kasse cash desk

kaste opp v vomit

kelner waiter

kilo kilo

kilometer kilometer

kino movie theater [cinema BE]

kirke church

kjedelig boring

kjemisk toalett chemical toilet

kjenne v know (somebody)

kjole dress

kjæreste boyfriend; girlfriend

kjøleskap refrigerator

kjøpe buy

kjøpesenter mall

kjøre v drive

kjørelengde mileage

klar ready

klassisk musikk classical
  music

klesbutikk clothing store

kleskode dress code

klimaanlegg air conditioning

klipp haircut

klippe n cliff; v cut
(with scissors)

klokke watch

klosettpumpe plunger

knipling lace

kniv knife

kobber copper

koffert suitcase

kokemuligheter cooking
facilities

kollega colleague

komfyr stove

komme v come

komme frem v arrive

komme til v get to

komme tilbake v return
(come back)

konditori pastry shop

kondom condom

kone wife

konferanse conference

konferansesenter convention hall

konsert concert

kontaktlinse contact lens

kontaktlinsevæske contact
lens solution

kontanter cash

konto account

kontor office

kontortid office hours

kontroll control

kopi print (photo)

kopp cup

korketrekker corkscrew

kort n card; adj short

koscher kosher

koste v cost

kredittkort credit card

krone krone
(Norwegian currency)

krystall crystal

kullsyrefri non-carbonated

kunne can; may

kurs rate (of exchange)

kveld evening

kvinne woman

kvittering receipt

kysse v kiss

kåpe coat (woman's)

L

la oss let's

la være i fred v leave alone

lag team

lage v make

lagre v save (computer)

laken sheet

laktoseintolerant lactose intolerant

land country; countryside

landekode country code

lang long

langbukser pants [trousers BE]

langsom slow

langsomt slowly

langt far

lappe v mend

lav low

lavhælt flat (shoe)

leddgikt arthritis

lege doctor

legemiddel medication

legge igjen v leave (deposit)

legitimasjon identification

leie v hire; rent

leiebil rental car

leilighet apartment

lekegrind playpen

lekeplass playground

leketøy toy

leketøysbutikk toy store

lett easy; light (weight)

leve v live

levende musikk live music

levere tilbake v return (give back)

lighter lighter

like v like

lin linen (cloth)

linje line (transport); extension (phone)

liten small

liter liter

litt little; some (with singular nouns)

livbåt life boat

logge seg av log off
logge seg inn log in
logge seg på log on
lokal local
lomme pocket
lommebok wallet
lunsj lunch
lusekofte cardigan (Norwegian)
lynmelder instant messenger
lys *n* light; *adj* light (color)
lysestake candlestick
lyspære light bulb
lær leather
løse inn *v* cash
løype trail [piste BE]
løypekart trail map
  [piste map BE]
lås lock
låse seg ute *v* lock oneself out

M

mage stomach
magesmerte stomachache
mange many
mangle *v* miss

manikyr manicure
mann man
marked market
maskin machine
maskinvaskbar machine
  washable
massasje massage
mat food
mate *v* feed
med with
meget very
melkeprodukter dairy
mellomstor medium
men but
menstruasjon period (monthly)
menstruasjonssmerter
  menstrual cramps
meny menu
mer more
messe mass (church)
meter meter
middag dinner (meal); noon
  [midday BE]
midnatt midnight
midt imot opposite

midtgang aisle

mikrobølgeovn microwave

mindre less

minibank ATM

minnebrikke memory card

minutt minute

miste *v* lose

mobil cell [mobile BE] phone

mokkasiner loafers

moms sales tax [VAT BE]

monter display case

moped moped

mopp mop

morgen morning

morsmelkerstatning formula

moské mosque

motorbåt motorboat

motorsykkel motorcycle

motorvei highway
[motorway BE]

motta *v* receive

mulig possible

munn mouth

museum museum

musikk music

mye much

mynt coin

mørk dark

møte meeting

møterom meeting room

møtes *v* meet

målebeger measuring cup

måleskje measuring spoon

måltid meal

måned month

måtte *v* must (have to)

N

narresmokk pacifier
[dummy BE] (baby's)

nasjonalpark nature preserve

natt night

natten over overnight

nattklubb nightclub

navn name

ned down

negl nail (human)

neglefil nail file

neglesalong nail salon

nei no

neste next

noe any; anything; something

noen anyone; some (with plural nouns); someone

nord north

Norge Norway

normalbensin regular (fuel)

norsk Norwegian

nummer number (counting); size (shoes)

ny new

nybegynner novice

nyte *v* enjoy

nær near

nærmeste nearest

nødutgang emergency exit

nøkkel key

nøkkelkort key card

nå *adv* now; *v* reach

når when

O

olabukser jeans

om ettermiddagen p.m. (afternoon)

om kvelden p.m. (evening)

om morgenen a.m.

ombordstigning boarding

ombordstigningskort boarding pass

område area; region

opera opera

oppbevaringsboks luggage locker

opptatt busy

oppvaskmaskin dishwasher

oppvaskmiddel dish detergent

optiker optician

ordbok dictionary

ostehøvel cheese slicer

overfall attack; mugging

overfalle *v* mug

oversette *v* translate

overvektig bagasje excess luggage

overveldende stunning

P

p-pille pill (contraceptive)

pakke package [parcel BE]; *v* pack

pakke inn *v* wrap up

palass palace
papir paper
papirkluter baby wipes
papirkopi av et digitalt bilde
  digital print
papirlommetørkle tissue
paracetamol acetaminophen
  [paracetamol BE]
paraply umbrella
parfyme perfume
parfymeri perfumery
park n park
parkere v park
parkeringsplass parking lot
  [car park BE]
pass passport
passe v fit
passende suitable
passkontroll passport control
passord password
peke v point
penger money
penicillin penicillin
penn pen
pensjonat guesthouse
pensjonert retired (from work)

pensjonist senior citizen
per dag per day
per kilometer per kilometer
per natt per night
per time per hour
per uke per week
perle pearl
perrong platform [BE] (station)
picnic picnic
pille pill
plage v bother
plaskebasseng kiddie
  [paddling BE] pool
plass place (hostel); seat;
  square
plaster bandage [plaster BE]
plastfolie plastic wrap
  [cling film BE]
plombe filling (tooth)
politi police
politirapport police report
politistasjon police station
popmusikk pop music
porsjon portion
post mail [post BE]
postkasse mailbox [postbox BE]

postkontor post office

postkort postcard

praktfull amazing

presentere *v* introduce (person)

presse *v* press (iron)

pris price

problem problem

protestantisk Protestant

prøve *v* try on

prøverom fitting room

pund pound (money)

puste *v* breathe

pute pillow

pyjamas pajamas

på on (place); to (time)

R

rabatt discount

racket racket (sport)

rane rob

rap rap (music)

rapport report

rask quick

regn *n* rain

regne *v* rain

regnfrakk raincoat

regnfull rainy

regning check [bill BE]
(restaurant)

reinsdyrskinn reindeer skin

reise *v* travel

reisebyrå travel agency

reisehåndbok travel guide

reisesjekk traveler's check
[cheque BE]

reisesyke motion sickness

ren clean

rengjøringsmidler cleaning
supplies

renseri dry cleaner

reparere *v* fix; repair

resept prescription

restaurant restaurant

retning direction

retningsnummer area code

rett dish (food); right (correct)

rett frem straight ahead

rimelig inexpensive

ring *n* ring (jewelry)

ringe *v* call (phone)

ringetid prepaid calling time

robåt rowboat

rolig quiet

rom room

romantisk romantic

romservice room service

rosa pink

ruin *n* ruin

rullestol wheelchair

rullestolsrampe wheelchair ramp

rulletrapp escalator

runde round (golf)

rundt around (nearby)

rute route

rutetabell schedule [timetable BE] (transportation)

rygg back (body part)

ryggsekk backpack

rød red

røyke *v* smoke

røykfri non-smoking (area)

safe *n* safe; *adj* trygg

saks scissors

salve cream (pharmaceutical)

samtale call (phone)

sandaler sandals

sanitetsbind sanitary napkin

savnet missing

se *v* look; see

seilbrett windsurfer

selge *v* sell

selvbetjeningsvaskeri laundromat [launderette BE]

seminar seminar

sen late

sende *v* send; ship

sende e-post *v* e-mail

senere later

seng bed

sentrum downtown area

separert separated

servere *v* serve

service service

serviett napkin

servitør waiter, waitress

sete ved midtgangen aisle seat

setning sentence

sette *v* put

sette inn *v* insert

sette over *v* put through

severdighet point of interest

shorts shorts

si *v* tell

side side

sigar cigar

sigarett cigarette

sightseeing sightseeing

sightseeingtur sightseeing tour

silke silk

sist last

sjampo shampoo

sjekk *n* check [cheque BE]

sjekke e-post *v* check e-mail

sjekke inn check in (airport)

sjekke ut check out

sjø sea

skade *v* damage

skatt tax

ski skis

skiheis ski lift

skilt divorced

skip ship

skitrekk drag lift

skitten dirty

skive slice

skje spoon

skjema form (document)

skjerf scarf

skjorte shirt

skjørt skirt

sko shoes

skobutikk shoe store

skog forest

skrive *v* write; type (computer)

skrive ut *v* print

skru av *v* turn off (device)

skru på *v* turn on (device)

skyve *v* push (open)

skål saucer; cheers (a toast)

slagsted battleground

sleiv spatula

slett *v* clear (ATM)

slette *v* delete (computer)

slott castle

slutt *n* end

slutte *v* end

smake *v* taste

smakløs bland

smerte pain

smykker jewelry

snakke *v* speak

snart soon

snorkleutstyr snorkeling equipment

snø *n/v* snow

snøbrett snowboard

sokk sock

sol sun

solbriller sunglasses

solforbrenning sunburn

solkrem sunscreen

solstikk sunstroke

sommer summer

spa spa

spasere *v* walk (stroll)

spesialitet speciality

spille *v* play

spille på hester *v* place a bet

spillehall arcade

spillkort playing card

spise *v* eat

spisekart menu (printed)

spor track (railway)

springvann tap water

sprinkelseng crib [child's cot BE]

språk language

spørre *v* ask

spørsmål question

stadion stadium

starte *v* start

stasjon station

staver poles (ski)

sted place

stekepanne frying pan

stemple stamp

stenge *v* close

stengt closed

sterlingsølv sterling silver

sti path
stikkontakt outlet (electric)
stjele v steal
stjålet stolen
stol chair
stolheis chair lift
stoppe v stop
stor big; large
stormagasin department store
storslagen magnificent
strand beach
strykejern iron (clothing)
strømpe stocking
strømpebukse panty hose [tights BE]
strømuttak electrical outlet
student student
studere v study
stuss trim (hair)
stygg ugly
stykke piece; play (theater)
style v style (hair)
større bigger
størrelse size (clothes)
støvel boot

støvsuger vacuum cleaner
sulten hungry
super premium; super (gasoline)
supermarked supermarket
surfebrett surfboard
surstoffbehandling oxygen treatment
suvenir souvenir
suvenirbutikk souvenir store
svart black
svelge v swallow
svimmel dizzy
svømme v swim
svømmebasseng swimming pool
syk sick [ill BE]
sykebil ambulance
sykeforsikring health insurance
sykehus hospital
sykepleier nurse
sykkel bicycle
sykkelløp cycling race
sykkelsti bike route
sykling cycling
synagoge synagogue

synshemmet visually impaired

sølv silver

søppel trash [rubbish BE]

søppelsekk garbage
  [rubbish BE] bag

sør south

søt cute

søvnighet drowsiness

såpe soap

sår hals sore throat

T

T-bane subway
  [underground BE]

T-banestasjon subway
  [underground BE] station

T-skjorte T-shirt

ta v take

ta med v bring (something)

ta med seg v take away (carry)

ta selv v help (oneself)

ta ut v withdraw (from account)

tablett tablet (medical)

takke v thank

tall number (counting)

tallerken plate

tampong tampon

tann tooth

tannlege dentist

tannbørste toothbrush

tannpasta toothpaste

tannpine toothache

taubane cable car

tegn symbol

tekst n text (message)

tekste v text (someone)

telefon phone

telefonkort phone card

telefonnummer phone number

telefonsamtale phone call

telt tent

tempel temple (religion)

tenke på v think about

tennis tennis

tennisbane tennis court

tenniskamp tennis match

terminal terminal (airport)

teskje teaspoon

tid time

til to (direction)

til until (time)

tilbake back (direction)

tilbehør accessories

tillate v permit

tillatt allowed

tiltrekkende attractive

time hour; lesson

ting thing

tinn pewter

titt look

toalett restroom [toilet BE]

toalettpapir toilet paper

tobakk tobacco

tobakkshandel tobacconist's

tog train

togtabell train schedule
[timetable BE]

tolk interpreter

toll customs; duty (tax)

tollfri duty-free

tom empty

topp peak

torg town square

tradisjonell traditional

trafikklys traffic light

trafikkskilt road sign

tralle cart (luggage)

trapp stairs

travbane racetrack
[race course BE]

treffe v see (meet)

trefigur wooden figurine

trekke v pull

trenge v need

treningsdrakt sweatsuit

trikk tram BE

trimrom gym

tro v think (believe)

truger snowshoes

trygg safe (free from danger)

trykk pressure

trøye undershirt

trådløst internett wireless
internet

tung heavy

tur tour; trip

tur-returbillett round-trip
[return BE] ticket

turistklasse economy class
turistkontor tourist office
turnsko sneakers
turområde picnic area
tursti walking route
TV TV
typisk typically
tyv thief
tyveri theft
tøfler slippers
tøm *v* empty
tørr *adj* dry
tåteflaske baby bottle

U

ugift single (unmarried)
uke week
ull wool
ullteppe blanket
ulykke accident
underlig strange
underrette *v* notify
undersøke *v* see (examine)
undertegne *v* sign

unnskylde *v* excuse
urolig mage upset stomach
uten without
utendørs svømmebasseng
  outdoor pool
utflukt excursion
utgang exit; gate
utleie hire
utsikt overlook
utsjekking check out
utslett rash
utstyr equipment
uttale *v* pronounce;
  n pronunciation
uvel nauseous

V

vakker beautiful
valuta currency
vandrerhjem youth hostel
vann water
vannscooter jet ski
vannski water skis
vanskelig difficult

vare goods

varm hot; warm

varme *n* heat [heating BE]; *v* warm

varmeovn heater

vask laundry (clothes)

vaskbar washable

vaske *v* clean; wash

vaskemaskin washing mashine

vaskemiddel detergent

vaskemuligheter laundry facilities

ved at

ved siden av next to

vegetarianer vegetarian

vei road

veikart road map

veikryss intersection

vekke *v* wake

vekking wake-up call

veksle *v* change (money); exchange

vekslepenger *n* change (money)

vekslingskontor currency exchange office

vekslingskurs exchange rate

velkommen welcome

venn friend

venstre left

vente *v* wait

vente på *v* wait for

verdi value

vest west

vifte fan (appliance)

vikingskip viking ship

viktig important

ville want to

vindu window

vindusplass window seat

vinkart wine list

vinmonopol liquor store [off-licence BE]

vinter winter

virke *v* work (function)

vise *v* show

visittkort business card

vite *v* know (something)

voldtekt rape

volleyballkamp volleyball game

vondt i brystet chest pain

vær så snill please

vær weather

være *v* be

værutsikter weather forecast

øye eye

øyeblikk moment

øyeblikkelig quickly

øyenbryn eyebrow

Ø

ørering earring

øreverk earache

øst east

Å

åpen *adj* open

åpne *v* open

år year